SPARKNOTES

Power Tactics

FOR THE NEW SAT

THE CRITICAL READING SECTION
SENTENCE COMPLETIONS

D0107177

SPARK
NOTES

A DIVISION OF BARNES & NOBLE PUBLISHING

SPARKNOTES is a registered trademark of SparkNotes LLC

Spark Educational Publishing
A Division of Barnes & Noble Publishing
120 Fifth Avenue
New York, NY 10011

ISBN 1-4114-0273-1

Please submit changes or report errors to *www.sparknotes.com/errors*.

Printed and bound in Canada.

SAT is the registered trademark of the College Entrance Examination Board, which was not involved in the production of, and does not endorse this product.

Written by Doug Tarnopol

CONTENTS

INTRODUCTION

Truly effective SAT preparation doesn't need to be painful or time consuming. SparkNotes' *Power Tactics for the New SAT* is proof that powerful test preparation can be streamlined so that you study only what you need. Instead of toiling away through a 700-page book or an expensive six-week course, you can choose the *Power Tactics* book that gets you where you want to be a lot sooner.

Perhaps you're Kid Math, the fastest number-slinger this side of the Mississippi, but a bit of a bumbler when it comes to words. Or maybe you've got the verbal parts down but can't seem to manage algebraic functions. SparkNotes' *Power Tactics for the New SAT* provides an extremely focused review of every component on the new SAT, so you can design your own program of study.

If you're not exactly sure where you fall short, log on to **testprep.sparknotes.com/powertactics** and take our free diagnostic SAT test. This test will pinpoint your weaknesses and reveal exactly where to focus.

Since you're holding this book in your hands, it's pretty likely that you need some test-taking strategies to guide your study and preparation for the SAT. You've made the right decision because in a few short hours, you will have mastered the art of taking the SAT. No sweat, no major investment of time or money, no problem.

So, let's not waste any time: go forth and conquer the SAT so you can get on with the *better parts* of your life!

ABOUT THE NEW SAT

THE OLD

The SAT, first administered in 1926, has undergone a thorough restructuring. For the last ten years, the SAT consisted of two sections: Verbal and Math. The Verbal section contained Analogies, Sentence Completions, and Critical Reading passages and questions. The Math section tested arithmetic, algebra, and geometry, as well as some probability, statistics and data interpretation.

You received one point for each correct answer. For most questions, a quarter of a point was deducted for each incorrect answer. This was called the "wrong-answer penalty," which was designed to neutralize random guessing. If you simply filled in the bubble sheet at random, you'd likely get one-fifth of the items correct, given that each item has five answer choices (excluding student-produced–response items). You'd also get four-fifths of the items wrong, losing $4 \times \frac{1}{4}$, or 1 point for the four incorrectly answered items. Every time you determined an answer choice was wrong, you'd improve your odds by beating the wrong-answer penalty. The net number of points (less wrong-answer penalties) was called the "raw score."

Raw score = # of correct answers – ($\frac{1}{4} \times$ # of wrong answers)

That score was then converted to the familiar 200–800 "scaled score."

THE NEW

For 2005, the SAT added a Writing section and an essay, changed the name of *Verbal* to *Critical Reading*, and added algebra II content to the Math section. The following chart compares the old SAT with the new SAT:

Old SAT	New SAT
Verbal	**Critical Reading**
Analogies	*Eliminated*
Sentence Completions	Sentence Completions
Long Reading Passages	Long Reading Passages
Paired Reading Passages	Paired Reading Passages
	Short Reading Passages
Math—Question Types	
Multiple Choice	Multiple Choice
Quantitative Comparisons	*Eliminated*
Student-produced Responses	Student-produced Responses
Math—Content Areas	
Numbers & Operations	Numbers & Operations
Algebra I	Algebra I
	Algebra II
Geometry	Geometry
Data Analysis, Statistics & Probability	Data Analysis, Statistics & Probability
	Writing
	Identifying Sentence Errors
	Improving Sentences
	Improving Paragraphs
	Essay
Total Time: 3 hours	*Total Time*: 3 hours, 45 minutes
Maximum Scaled Score: 1600	*Maximum Scaled Score*: 2400 Separate Essay Score (2–12)

The scoring for the test is the same, except that the Writing section provides a third 200–800 scaled score, and there is now a separate essay score. The wrong-answer penalty is still in effect.

NEW PACKAGE, OLD PRODUCT

While the test has changed for test-*takers*, it has not changed all that much from the test-*maker*'s point of view. The Educational Testing Service (ETS) is a nonprofit institute that creates the SAT for The College Board. Test creation is not as simple a task as you might think. Any standardized test question has to go through a rigorous series of editorial reviews and statistical studies before it can be released to the public. In fact, that's why the old SAT featured a seventh, unscored, "experimental" section: new questions were tested out in these sections. ETS "feeds" potential questions to its test-takers in order to measure the level of difficulty. Given the complex and lengthy process of developing new questions, it would be impossible for ETS to introduce *totally* new question types or make major changes to existing question types.

Now that you know these facts, the "new" SAT will start to make more sense. The changes were neither random nor unexpected. Actually, the only truly *new* question type on the SAT is the short reading passages followed by a couple of questions. However, the skills tested and strategies required are virtually identical to the tried-and-true long reading passage question type. All other additions to the test consist of new *content* rather than new *question types*. Both multiple-choice and student-produced–response math questions ("grid-ins") will now feature algebra II concepts. Same question type, new content. Critical Reading features one fiction passage as well as questions on genre, rhetorical devices, and cause and effect. Same question type, different content.

Even the much-feared Writing section is, in a sense, old news. Both the PSAT and the SAT II Writing test have featured exactly the same multiple-choice question types for years. The essay format and scoring rubric will be virtually identical to that of the SAT II Writing Test. The College Board had no other choice, given how long the test-development process is.

The other major changes are omissions, not additions: Quantitative Comparisons and Analogies have been dumped from the test.

So in a nutshell, ETS has simply attached an SAT II Writing test to the old SAT, dropped Analogies and Quantitative Comparisons, added in some algebra II content and short reading passages, and ensured that some fiction and fiction-related questions were included. That's it.

A USER'S GUIDE

Reading this book will provide you with powerful tools to maximize your score on Sentence Completions. We've divided up your study into two sections: **Power Tactics** and **Practice Sets**. The Power Tactics will provide you with important concepts and strategies you'll need to tackle Sentence Completions. The Practice Sets will give you an opportunity to apply what you learn to SAT questions. To achieve your target score, you'll learn:

- The three basic Sentence Completions you'll encounter
- What the test-makers are actually trying to test with Sentence Completions
- Essential concepts and powerful step methods to maximize your score
- Test-taking strategies that allow you to approach each section with the best possible mindset
- The 6 most common mistakes and how to avoid them

We will show you how to use the skills you already have to get more points. With that knowledge, you will learn our two major step methods for mastering Sentence Completions, with ample opportunity for guided and independent practice.

In order to get the most out of this book:

- Make sure to read each section thoroughly and carefully.
- Don't skip the Guided Practice questions.
- Read all explanations to all questions.
- Go to **testprep.sparknotes.com/powertactics** for a free full-length diagnostic **pretest**. This test will help you determine your strengths and weaknesses for Sentence Completions and for the entire SAT.
- Go back to our website after you complete this book to take a **posttest**. This test will tell you how well you've mastered Sentence Completions and what topics you still need to review.

Look upon this book as your personal trainer. If you stick with the training program, you'll reach your full potential.

THE POWER
TACTICS

ANATOMY OF A SENTENCE COMPLETION

In this section, we provide you with an X-ray of Sentence Completions. By looking at these questions inside and out, you'll know more about how The College Board tests your skills and how to approach each and every Sentence Completion you'll encounter on the SAT.

Here is a typical Sentence Completion and the terms we'll use to refer to its various parts:

1. In the Middle Ages, when few women held true political power, the irrepressible Eleanor of Aquitaine ------- England while her son, Richard the Lionhearted, tramped through Europe and the Middle East on the First Crusade.

(A) domesticated
(B) ruled
(C) destroyed
(D) betrayed
(E) repressed

The sentence containing the blank is the **stem**. The lettered options below the stem are called the **answer choices**. One of these—choice **B**—is correct; the other four answer choices are called **distractors** because that's exactly what they're designed to do: *distract* attention from the correct answer. The stem and answer choices grouped together are called an **item**.

Sentence Completions test sentence-level reading skills, as well as vocabulary. As you'll learn, context clues are at least as important as vocabulary knowledge. There are many such clues in this example:

1. The phrase *when few women held true political power* tells you what the general rule was for medieval women.
2. The word *irrepressible*, meaning "impossible to repress or hold back," sets up Eleanor of Aquitaine as an exception to the general rule. At this point in your reading, you have at least a vague idea that Eleanor actually managed to gain some real power.
3. As you continue reading, you see that Eleanor's son, the King of England, spent his reign mostly out of the country. Who was minding the store, then? Eleanor. So, the correct answer is **B**, *ruled*.

We simplified the vocabulary in this item so that you would pay attention to the anatomy of Sentence Completion items. Our goal is that you start to understand how the steps listed above are typical of the kind of automatic process you already use to figure out words in sentences, a process called "reading."

THE PLAIN-OLD SENTENCE

You know more than you think you do. This section will prove that. A large part of preparing for Sentence Completions is unearthing the methods you already use to comprehend language and one of its most basic elements: the sentence.

On the SAT, most Sentence Completion stems are one of three basic types. Other types occur, including items that are "definitional," but if you learn to recognize and handle the three basic stem types, you'll have acquired the tools you will need to tackle any potential Sentence Completion item.

Consider the following sentence:

> The drummer's playing was so loud that the other instruments couldn't be heard above the din.

What's going on here? It's a simple cause-and-effect relationship: loud drumming drowns out other musicians. The effect, drowning out other musicians, follows directly from the cause, loud drumming. Next, consider this sentence:

> Although the drummer played loudly, the other instruments were clearly audible.

This sentence has a twist. Something exceptional is implied: drummer plays loudly, but other instruments can still be heard. Finally, look at the following sentence:

> At first merely loud, the drummer's playing rose to deafening levels as the concert progressed, drowning out all other instruments.

In this sentence, what was loud at first soon becomes deafening. The sentence, as well as the drumming it describes, has been amplified.

These three sentences represent the three major types of Sentence Completion stems:

- **Continuation**
- **Contrast**
- **Amplification**

There are typical context clues associated with each type, which we'll point out in a later section. At this point, we just want you to appreciate how knowing about these three typical stem types already gives your test performance a boost. Much as a shark will attack anything it perceives as "fish-like," you now have a "search image" that can help focus your attack by helping you predict and recognize correct answers.

THE SENTENCE COMPLETION

Sentence Completions work as follows:

1. Each stem has one or two blanks, which indicate missing a word or short phrase.
2. Each item has five answer choices that supply words or short phrases for those omissions.
3. One of these choices provides the *best* fit within the sentence's meaning when plugged into the sentence.

The key word in this last point is *best*. English does not have the all-or-nothing precision of mathematics. Distractors may be anything from entirely nonsensical to insufficiently clear, but the correct answer will be the best answer of the lot, if not the best possible word.

Sentence Completion items on the new SAT are presented in order of difficulty. These items are scored as follows: one point for every correctly answered item, a quarter-point off for every incorrectly answered item, and no points for every unanswered item. The easiest items are listed first; the hardest are listed last. We'll discuss how you can strategically use the order of difficulty in a later section.

Let's return to our three stem types with our example sentences:

- **Continuation:***The drummer's playing was so loud that the other instruments couldn't be heard above the din.*
- **Contrast:***Although the drummer played loudly, the other instruments were clearly audible.*
- **Amplification:***At first merely loud, as the concert progressed, the drummer's playing rose to deafening levels, drowning out all other instruments.*

The following sections will demonstrate how each of the example sentences could be turned into a one- and a two-blank item, starting with the *continuation* sentence.

Continuation

3. The drummer's playing was so ------- that the other instruments couldn't be heard above the din.

(A) quiet
(B) poor
(C) loud
(D) enthusiastic
(E) fast

If the drummer's playing drowned out the other instruments, then it must have been *loud*. **C** is the correct answer. **A** is the opposite of what's required. The other choices present other possible qualities of the drummer's playing, but none have anything to do with the other instruments' ability to be *heard*.

Here's a two-blank version of the *continuation* sentence:

7. The drummer's playing was so ------- that the other instruments couldn't be ------- above the din.

(A) quiet . . played
(B) poor . . appreciated
(C) loud . . heard
(D) enthusiastic . . ignored
(E) fast . . discerned

This one's harder. Two-blank items tend to be harder since they contain more unknowns and usually require greater insight into sentence structure than is necessary for one-blank items. However, there are brutal one-blank items that test difficult vocabulary. Two-blank items, such as the previous example, also depend on vocabulary knowledge. If you don't know what *din* means, for example, this item will be a bit more challenging.

Choice **A** doesn't make any sense—what would quiet drumming have to do with the ability to play the other instruments? And what would that have to do with *din*? Those who don't know what *din* means still have a shot at eliminating **A** on common sense alone. **B** is one of those nasty distractors that separate those who grasp the stem's structure but don't know what *din* means from those who grasp both the structure and *din*'s meaning. One could picture poor drumming ruining a listener's appreciation for the other instruments, but this sentence is about loudness. **D**'s first word fits the first part of the stem, but what does enthusiastic playing have to do with something the other instruments couldn't accomplish due to the *din*? Finally, **E** makes a leap from *fast* drumming to causing a *din*, which is not necessarily true. The drummer could be playing quickly *and* quietly. So, you can see why **C** is the best answer.

Contrast

Here's a one-blank version for the contrast sentence:

2. Although the drummer played -------, the other instruments were clearly audible.

(A)   quietly
(B)   poorly
(C)   loudly
(D)   enthusiastically
(E)   quickly

Note how in contrast sentences, you have to work backward. On its own, *Although the drummer played* ------- gives insufficient information. But the word *although* warns you that the drummer's playing will contrast with the effect conveyed by the second part of the sentence.

There are many words that stand for contrast; others stand for continuation. Here's a handy chart:

Continuation	Contrast
also, and, as well as, because, since, therefore, thus	although, but, despite, even though, however, yet

In the second part of the sentence, *the other instruments were clearly audible,* the last word gives you the vocabulary clue you need. *Audible* means "able to be heard," so how must the drummer have been playing to make the audibility of the other instruments surprising? What would complete the "twist"? **A** certainly won't—why use *Although* if the expected cause-and-effect relationship occurred? **B, D,** and **E** provide potential descriptions of the drummer's playing, but none of them would have an impact on the other instruments' audibility, let alone in the surprising manner that would complete the "twist."

A two-blank version of this sentence could look like this:

10. Although the drummer played -------, the other instruments were clearly -------.

(A)   quietly . . missing
(B)   poorly . . ignored
(C)   loudly . . audible
(D)   enthusiastically . . unappreciated
(E)   quickly . . synchronized

Again, this one's tougher than the one-blank version. In the one-blank version, *audible* was the critical piece that led to the correct choice. Here, it's missing from the stem, although *clearly* gives you a subtle clue. This item tests common sense as well as the vocabulary in the answer choices. **A** creates an unclear sentence. What would quiet drumming have to do with the physical absence of the other instruments? In **B**, poor playing is associated with ignoring other instruments, which doesn't necessarily follow. Choice **D** could work if *Although* were *Because*—in our terms, if this were a continuation, rather than a contrast, sentence. **E** is a little tricky because it encourages a rushed test-taker to accept that the drummer's fast playing didn't throw off his fellow band members. But the actual meaning is a bit unclear. Were the other instruments clearly synchronized with each other? With the drummer? Both? Remember, the instructions ask you to select the answer that *best* completes the sentence. **E** is clearly not the *best* completion of the sentence; **C** is.

Amplification

Finally, let's look at the amplification sentence as a one-blank and a two-blank item:

3. At first merely -------, the drummer's playing rose to deafening levels as the concert progressed, drowning out all other instruments.

(A)   quiet
(B)   poor
(C)   loud
(D)   enthusiastic
(E)   fast

Does **A** best complete the sentence? Which word suggests that it doesn't? Yes, *merely* is the kicker here. It's possible that the drummer started out playing quietly and later became deafening, but if that were the case, we wouldn't say *merely quiet*. *Merely* implies that the sound level was on the loud side to begin with, which is what **C** correctly provides. As in previous versions of this sentence, **B**, **D**, and **E** provide descriptions of drumming that have nothing to do with the sound level, and don't necessarily relate. They each could be true, but neither *poor* nor *enthusiastic* nor *fast* drumming is quite the same as *loud*; each merely suggests *loud* playing, whereas **C** comes right out and explicitly draws the connection between initial and subsequently deafening loudness.

A two-blank version of this *amplification* example could take the following form:

9. At first merely -------, the drummer's playing rose to ------- levels as the concert progressed, drowning out all other instruments.

(A)   quiet . . inaudible
(B)   poor . . virtuosic
(C)   loud . . deafening
(D)   enthusiastic . . ecstatic
(E)   fast . . rapid

We can see that something about the drummer's playing was amplified as the concert progressed. **A** presents an "amplified pair": *inaudible* means "quiet to the point of silence." This fits the bare logic of the sentence but misses on meaning. The last phrase, *drowning out all other instruments*, lets you know that you need a pair of words that signify loudness, which **C** provides. The words in **B** are opposites. Why would anyone use *merely* to describe a change from *poor* to *virtuosic* drumming—*virtuosic* meaning "expert?" If the first word were *competent*, then **B** would fit. But the last phrase tells us that loudness, not skill, is being discussed. Choice **D** also provides an "amplified pair," as *ecstasy* is an extreme form of *enthusiasm*. But the last phrase requires a pair of words describing loudness, not enthusiasm. Finally, **E** provides two words that are at the same "level," so to speak. What's faster: *fast* or *rapid*? It's hard to answer that question, right? Also, speed is not necessarily the same thing as loudness, as we've seen.

Sentence Completions test more than just vocabulary. They are critical reading items that test your understanding of basic sentence structure. Knowing that the SAT tests certain types of sentences, and knowing how those sentences behave, will help you gain points and predict how to fill in the blanks.

To review:

- **Continuation** sentences show a cause-and-effect relationship between their parts.
- **Contrast** sentences contain a "twist." Something surprising occurs within the sentence.
- **Amplification** sentences present an idea or description that grows in magnitude—bigger, smaller, louder, quieter.

Keep these typical sentence types in mind as you work through the forward and backward methods presented in the next section and as you work through the practice sets.

ESSENTIAL STRATEGIES

If you took the SAT cold, you'd still get some Sentence Completions right. But you probably wouldn't get those points in the most efficient way possible. Plus, there are many items you might skip, items you'll find a lot more approachable with just a little coaching and some simple strategies.

We'd like to present two methods you can use to solve Sentence Completions. The first is the "forward" method. This is an explicit discipline you should follow *every time* you attempt a Sentence Completion. The second is the "backward" method. You'll use this method when you can't successfully use the forward method.

THE FORWARD METHOD

Here are the five steps to the forward method:

Step 1: Cover up answer choices.

Step 2: Read stem and determine stem type.

Step 3: Supply your own words or phrases to complete the sentence.

Step 4: Compare your choice to the answers and eliminate all that do not match.

Step 5: Plug selected answer back into sentence and select the best fit.

You'll need to get your hands on a 3 × 5 index card and use it to cover up the answer choices from now on. Why? Because four of them are distractors, and you've already had a taste of what those are like. These exist to seduce you away from the correct answer. Covering up the answer choices decreases the "noise" of distractors and gives you a chance to figure out what kind of "signal" you're looking for.

In step 2, you'll determine whether the sentence is Continuation, Contrast, Amplification, or some other less common subtype. As you'll see, this choice will help you determine which words or phrases could complete the sentence. Armed with this signal, you're ready to consider the answer choices. Eliminate all that do not match your prediction. That will leave you with only one answer, but make sure to plug that choice's word or words into the sentence before you move on. If not, plug all remaining choices back into the stem and choose the one that fits best.

We'll show you how to tackle an item using this method. Then you'll get a chance to follow the method on your own.

The Forward Method in Slow Motion

We'd like to take you through the forward method in slow motion to demonstrate exactly how it works.

Consider the following item:

4. Some ethical philosophers argue that when the term "genocide" is used too liberally, the concept becomes -------, losing its power to mobilize international support for those ethnicities whose existence is truly endangered by mass murder.

Step 1: Cover up answer choices.

We've covered up the answer choices for you. Very smart and experienced people called "psychometricians" spend a lot of time designing distractors to hide the correct answer. Multiple-choice items always display the correct answer; distractors are there to camouflage it.

Step 2: Read stem and determine stem type.

Is this Continuation, Contrast, or Amplification? Well, we don't see any contrast clue words (e.g., *although, despite*, etc.), so it looks like we have a straightforward cause-and-effect Continuation sentence. You can translate the stem into "headline-speak" to clarify cause and effect: "Overuse of the term *genocide* leads to something that means a loss of the term's power."

This Sentence Completion also has a typical feature: the concluding phrase limits what words could reasonably fill in the blank. In some cases, the blank is actually *defined* by the final phrase, which is set off by a comma. Since the test-makers are testing your ability to use context to determine meaning, they "plant" context clues in Sentence Completions, even if they come off as slightly artificial. You, the test-taker, need to take advantage of this fact.

Step 3: Supply your own words or phrases to complete the sentence.

Now that we understand the sentence's logic, we can supply our own word to fill in the blank. What word means a loss of an entity's power? You don't need to get fancy—remember, you're under strict time constraints. How about *weak*? That would fit. Let's go with that for now. Using *weak* as your "search image" will certainly help us separate the wheat from the chaff when we look at the answer choices.

Step 4: Compare your choice to the answers and eliminate all that do not match.

Armed with your proposed answer, you're now ready to look at the answer choices:

4. Some ethical philosophers argue that when the term "genocide" is used too liberally, the concept becomes [weak], losing its power to mobilize international support for those ethnicities whose existence is truly endangered by mass murder.

    (A) conservative
    (B) militaristic
    (C) domestic
    (D) scarce
    (E) diluted

Which of the choices match *weak*? The only choices that have a shot are **D** and **E**. But let's take a look at the distractors so you can see the advantage of approaching the answer choices with a "search image." **A**, *conservative*, is a typically tricky choice, since in the heat of battle, the test-taker will see the word *liberally* and reach for its political opposite. However, *liberally* means "generously" in this context, so **A** is incorrect. The sentence also contains the word *mobilize*, which brings to·mind the movement of armed forces, which you might think is necessary to prevent genocide. Remember, though, Sentence Completions test vocabulary *in context*. If you select **B**, you're saying that the term "genocide" *itself* becomes militaristic if it's used too often. This doesn't make much sense. Choice **C** plays a similar associative game with another word in the stem. *Domestic* is paired with *international*, which may seem attractive to a test-taker who is strapped for time.

In fact, it's best to think of distractors as engaging in a lot of hand-waving, saying, "Choose me—hurry up! I'm close enough, and you're running out of time!" If you haven't figured out the type of stem you're dealing with or supplied a plausible word to fill in the blank, the distractors' power increases. Look how **D** does it—*scarce* plays off of *endangered* in the last phrase, laying a trap for careless test-takers. When you think about it, how could a term that is too liberally applied become scarce? Only **E**, *diluted*, captures the sense of a loss of the term's power. Even if you had no idea what *diluted* means, you'd still get this item right if you had stuck to your guns and eliminated those choices that do not match *weak*.

Step 5: Plug selected answer back into sentence and select the best fit.

As a final check, plug your selected choice into the stem: *Some ethical philosophers argue that when the term "genocide" is used too liberally, the concept becomes diluted, losing its power to mobilize international support for those ethnicities whose existence is truly endangered by mass murder.* Why bother with this step when you're in a hurry? Because accuracy is as important as speed, and choices can look very attractive until you've plugged them back into their stems. Skip this step, and you risk a 1 $^1/_4$-point turnaround: you'll not only lose the point you might have gained, but you'll also be docked a quarter-point.

Guided Practice

Try this one on your own:

3. Ignoring criticisms that the film was excessively ------- and biased, the director resisted efforts to cut particular scenes in order to produce a less fierce, more ------- story.

Step 1: Cover up answer choices.

We've taken care of this for you, but make sure you always cover up answer choices with an index card or whatever else is handy.

Step 2: Read stem and determine stem type.

This may look like a sentence with a "twist" until you study it a bit. The director ignored criticisms that the film was excessively *whatever it was*, specifically refusing to cut scenes that would have made the film both less than *whatever it was* and more than *the opposite of whatever it was*. Thus, *whatever it was* has remained the same.

Write down what kind of stem type this is here: _____

Step 3: Supply your own words or phrases to complete the sentence.

You will see there is another class of context clues in this item. The units [------- *and biased*] and [*less fierce, more* -------]. mirror each other. The first blank should match *fierce*; the second blank should match *biased*.

Write your candidates here:

First blank: _____

Second blank: _____

Step 4: Compare your choice to the answers and eliminate all that do not match.

Here are the answer choices:

(A)   placid . . prejudicial
(B)   tranquil . . neutral
(C)   brutal . . unfair
(D)   violent . . even-handed
(E)   long . . compact

Use the chart below to help you eliminate answer choices. If you don't know the meaning of the words in an answer choice, **don't** eliminate that answer choice. It might be the correct choice.

Your candidate for the first blank: _____

(A)   placid
(B)   tranquil
(C)   brutal
(D)   violent
(E)   long

(You probably eliminated at least one choice on the basis of your candidate. Cross out those choices below: why waste precious time evaluating the second word in a choice you've already eliminated? Also: you don't necessarily have to start with the first blank; you could start with the second, if that promises to be easier or quicker.)

Your candidate for the second blank: _____

(A)   prejudicial
(B)   neutral
(C)   unfair
(D)   even-handed
(E)   compact

Step 5: Plug selected answer back into sentence and select the best fit.

Don't forget to do this, even if you've whittled down the choices to one.

Write your answer here: _____

Guided Practice Explanation

Did you come up with **D**? If so, congratulations! If not, don't worry—let's trace the thought process. Those who came up with **D** should follow along as well. The goal here is not to get this one item correct but to see how the thought processes in the step method work in action.

Step 1: Cover up answer choices.

Done for us.

Step 2: Read stem and determine stem type.

This sentence has neither a twist nor amplification. The units mirror each other, so this is a Continuation stem. Knowing this should help you predict what's needed to fill the blanks—you need a synonym for *fierce* and an antonym for *biased*.

Step 3: Supply your own words or phrases to complete the sentence.

Given that the units [------- *and biased*] and [*less fierce, more* -------] should mean the same thing (a common feature of Sentence Completions), we offer the following candidates:

First blank: brutal

Second blank: impartial

Note how the equivalency is complicated by the *less...*, *more...* construction. The second blank has to be the **opposite** of *biased* to preserve the sentence's logic.

Step 4: Compare your choice to the answers and eliminate all that do not match.

Our candidate for the first blank: brutal

- (A)   placid
- (B)   tranquil
- (C)   brutal
- (D)   violent
- (E)   long

In one fell swoop, our candidate has disqualified **A**, **B**, and **E**.

Our candidate for the second blank: impartial

- (C)   unfair
- (D)   even-handed

D is the only option left; **C** doesn't match our candidate.

Step 5: Plug selected answer back into sentence and select the best fit.

Ignoring criticisms that the film was excessively violent and biased, the director resisted efforts to cut particular scenes in order to produce a less fierce, more even-handed story.

Write your answer here: **D**

Whenever you practice, you should force yourself to follow this method. You don't need our help for those items you know off the top of your head. You need us at the "margins" of your knowledge, ability, and speed. That's where you'll raise the ceiling of your score, and that's where this method will help you deploy your knowledge as efficiently as possible.

THE BACKWARD METHOD

We said earlier that half of conquering Sentence Completions was recognizing and practicing an explicit method based on the multiple-choice nature of the item. But what do you do when you can't figure out the logic of a complex sentence? Or when you can't come up with a word to fill the blank quickly? Do you just give up? No, you go to the backward method, which represents the other half of conquering Sentence Completions. The method covers three common scenarios:

- **Scenario 1.** You can determine the stem type, but you can't come up with words to fill the blanks.
- **Scenario 2.** You've determined the stem type and have supplied words to fill the blanks, but you don't recognize any of the vocabulary in the answer choices.
- **Scenario 3.** You can't determine the stem type or supply words to fill the blanks.

In all the lists that follow, it's assumed that you've already covered up the answer choices and have read the stem.

The Backward Method: Scenario 1 in Slow Motion

You can determine the stem type, but you can't come up with words to fill the blanks.

Step 1: Use positive or negative signs to determine what type of word you'll need.

Step 2: Go to the answer choices and assign positive or negative signs to each word.

Step 3: Eliminate the choices that don't fit, then select from the rest.

Step 4: Plug your choice back into the stem as a check.

If you can't supply a specific word, you don't need to give up. Knowing whether you need a "positive" or "negative" word provides a less precise but still useful "search image." Look at the following item, which you encountered in a previous section:

4. Some ethical philosophers argue that when the term "genocide" is used too liberally, the concept becomes -------, losing its power to mobilize international support for those ethnicities whose existence is truly endangered by mass murder.

Let's say you couldn't come up with a word to fill the blank. Would you need a "positive" or "negative" word here? The concept clearly *loses* power when used too much, so you need a negative word of some kind. Now, look how this helps you when you consider the answer choices:

(A)   conservative
(B)   militaristic
(C)   domestic
(D)   scarce
(E)   diluted

Which of these is negative, in the sense of "lessening?" Judging whether **A** is positive or negative depends on the person doing the judging, so *conservative* isn't a particularly negative word in this context. It's probably not the right answer, so eliminate it. *Militaristic* suffers a bit from **A**'s difficulties, but it's probably negative enough for our purposes. Keep **B**. *Domestic* is certainly not negative. It doesn't seem very positive, either—and words with neutral connotations can be used as a third category in the backward method. But we need a clearly negative word to complete this item. **D** and **E** work. At this point, you've eliminated two options, so you're ahead of the game. You have a 1-in-3 shot at getting a point and a 2-in-3 shot of losing a quarter-point. Those are good odds over several items, so plug each choice into the sentence to see which "sounds" better, and choose that one.

Your Ear

A note on using your ear. Your "ear" is the way you use common sense to decipher language. Your ear's reliability depends on how much exposure to Standard Written English you've had. Nevertheless, we've all had *some* exposure and we know that slang is off limits on the SAT. So you can use your ear to hedge your bets.

In fact, "bet-hedging" is what the backward method is all about. Without this method, you have only a small chance (20 percent, actually) of getting a point when you're stuck. The wrong-answer penalty is designed to neutralize *random* guessing only. With the backward method, you raise your chances of getting a point by eliminating answer choices and guessing from what remains. Remember, you should guess whenever you can eliminate even one answer choice with a reasonable degree of confidence.

The Backward Method: Scenario 2 in Slow Motion

You've determined the stem type and have supplied words to fill the blanks, but you don't recognize any of the vocabulary in the answer choices.

Step 1: Apply "deciphering techniques" to the vocabulary in the answer choices.

Step 2: Plug each of the choices into the sentence, "listening" for which choices sound best.

Step 3: Plug your choice back into the stem as a check.

Some Sentence Completions use very tough vocabulary in the answer choices. In fact, one-blank items that appear later on in a set usually feature brutally difficult vocabulary. Look at this example:

10. The newly recognized amoral ------- of the natural world, which was traditionally seen as reflecting an ultimately benevolent purpose, was Darwin's most controversial intellectual legacy, generating strong reactions from those who wanted to preserve Nature's supposed ratification of Christian eschatology.

(A) stochasticity
(B) malevolence
(C)   determinism
(D) progressiveness
(E) contingency

Yes, this is a tough one. Even if you figure out that this is a complex version of a Continuation stem, and that you need a word that means "purposelessness," you still have to deal with those nasty answer choices. Here's where you can use "deciphering techniques."

Can you do anything with **A**? Unlikely, so don't eliminate it. It might be the correct answer. Look at **B**, *malevolence*. The prefix *mal-* means "bad"; the root *vol* means "will," as in the word, *volition*. So, *malevolence* should mean something like "ill will." Is that what you need to balance out *benevolent purpose*? Perhaps; perhaps not. But at least now you know what you're dealing with in choice **B**. The blank is actually contrasted with *purpose*, which is modified by *amoral*. Similarly, you may not be familiar with *determinism* as a philosophical concept, but you might know what *determined* means in the sense of "ordained." That's actually the opposite of what you want, so cut **C**.

Progressiveness may be unfamiliar, but "progress" is certainly more familiar. Since *-ness* refers to a "state of being," does a word that means "a state of being progressive" work? As in **C**, this doesn't really match "purposelessness," so eliminate **D**. *Contingency* may stump you, but have you ever heard a form of this word in another context? Half-remembered phrases can help you. If you'd ever heard a sentence like, "getting this scholarship is contingent upon scoring in at least the 90th percentile on the SAT," then you'd have a shot at deciphering this word's meaning. It seems to mean that certain outcomes are not guaranteed but rather depend upon certain prior events: score in the 90th percentile, get the scholarship. Does this match "purposelessness?" It just might—keep **E**. Read both **A** and **E** into the stem and choose the one that best fits. You're down to a 50/50 chance to either gain a point or lose a quarter-point, so you're well ahead of the wrong-answer penalty.

(By the way, **E** is correct: *The newly recognized amoral contingency of the natural world, which was traditionally seen as reflecting an ultimately benevolent purpose, was Darwin's most controversial intellectual legacy, generating strong reactions from those who wanted to preserve Nature's supposed ratification of Christian eschatology. Contingency* means "the state of being dependent on or conditioned by something else; not necessitated." *Stochasticity*, however, means "random or involving chance or probability," which is not exactly right in this context. After Darwin, nature was seen as neither progressive nor purposeful, but it was not seen as *entirely random. Eschatology*, incidentally, means "a branch of theology concerning the ultimate destiny of mankind or of the world.")

The Backward Method: Scenario 3 in Slow Motion
You can't determine the stem type or supply words to fill the blanks.

Step 1: Plug each of the choices into the sentence, "listening" for which choices sound better.

Step 2: Eliminate any that don't fit; choose from the remaining.

Step 3: Plug your choice back into the stem as a check.

Even if you're unsure of whether you need a positive or negative word, you may still be able to eliminate some answer choices based on your ear alone. Also, sometimes inserting the right (or clearly wrong) answer illuminates the stem's structure. Clearly, since you're at the mercy of the distractors, this method is a last-ditch effort to decide whether or not to omit an item.

Guided Practice

Try the following item, but avoid using the forward method. Instead, practice the backward method:

8. Globalization has not been the unmitigated ------- for global poverty that its more starry-eyed supporters promised; in fact, many would argue that globalization has not just failed to ------- want, it has even sharpened its bite.

(We'll assume that you've covered up the answer choices.) It's not immediately clear what kind of sentence this is. Note that a typical feature of difficult Sentence Completions is the repetition of negatives that confuse the logic: *Globalization has **not** been the **unmitigated** ------- for global poverty that its more starry-eyed supporters promised; in fact, many would argue that globalization has **not** just **failed** to ------- want, it has even sharpened its bite.*

Step 1. Use positive or negative signs to determine what type of word
       you'll need.

Given how tortuous the stem's logic is, using positive and negative signs instead of word choices might help, especially since difficult vocabulary in the answer choices often accompanies convoluted stems.

Write a plus or minus sign next to each named blank below:
First Blank: _____
Second Blank: _____

Step 2. Go to the answer choices and assign positive or negative signs to
       each word.

The answer choices are listed below.

(A)   disaster . . increase
(B)   mediation . . alleviate
(C)   boon . . exacerbate
(D)   calamity . . reduce
(E)   panacea . . ameliorate

Now, assign positive or negative signs to each of the first words in each answer choice.

Reproduce the sign you gave the first blank here: _____

(A)   disaster
(B)   mediation
(C)   boon
(D)   calamity
(E)   panacea

Reproduce the sign you gave the second blank here: _____

(A)   increase
(B)   alleviate
(C)   exacerbate
(D)   reduce
(E)   ameliorate

Step 3. Eliminate those pairs that don't fit; select from the rest.

You may do this by crossing off all those that don't fit in the lists above.

Step 4. Plug your choice back into the stem as a check.

Always do this, even if you're only left with one answer.

Write your answer here: _____

Guided Practice Explanation

What did you come up with? Compare it to the following explanation. Pay attention to the thought process and method used, rather than the ultimate answer.

8.   Globalization has not been the unmitigated ------- for global poverty that its more starry-eyed supporters promised; in fact, many would argue that globalization has not just failed to ------- want, it has even sharpened its bite.

Step 1. Use positive or negative signs to determine what type of word you'll need.

This is a complex sentence. There was some promised association between globalization and global poverty, but what was it? One key is the adjective *starry-eyed*, which means "utopian or overly favorable." The other key is the use of *want* in the second part of the sentence, meaning "poverty." Work through the logic: if globalization's true believers were overly favorable, they probably were promising that globalization would reduce global poverty. If globalization was expected to decrease poverty, then it was expected to be an *unmitigated* positive of some kind (*unmitigated* means "not lessened").

Now, look at the second blank. Globalization has not reduced poverty. Thus, it has failed to make *want*, or poverty, any better. This part of the sentence is a bit more complicated, as it brings in a "*not just...it has even*" construction, which is similar to "*not only...but also.*" If *want's* bite has been *sharpened*, then there's deeper poverty than before. So, you actually need a **positive** word for this blank to stand for what globalization **failed** to accomplish.

Write a plus or minus sign next to each named blank below:

First Blank: +

Second Blank: +

Step 2. Go to the answer choices and assign positive or negative signs to each word.

The answer choices are listed below.

(A)   disaster . . increase
(B)   mediation . . alleviate
(C)   boon . . exacerbate
(D)   calamity . . reduce
(E)   panacea . . ameliorate

Now, assign positive or negative signs to each of the first words in each answer choice.

Reproduce the sign you gave the first blank here: +

Write a positive or negative sign next to each of the following words:

(A)   disaster –
(B)   mediation +
(C)   boon +
(D)   calamity –
(E)   panacea +

You've eliminated two choices as most likely being wrong. Of course, this determination depends on whether you know enough about the meaning of each word in order to assign a positive or negative sign to each of them. But you don't need as precise a grasp on meaning when you use signs as you do when you supply a candidate word to fill in the blank. That's the power of this method.

Reproduce the sign you gave the second blank here: +

Write a positive or negative sign next to each of the following words:

(B)   alleviate +
(C)   exacerbate –
(E)   ameliorate +

Step 3. Eliminate those pairs that don't fit; select from the rest.

We've done that above. We're left with either **B** or **E**.

Step 4. Plug your choice back into the stem as a check.

Which sounds better?

> Globalization has not been the unmitigated mediation for global poverty that its more starry-eyed supporters promised; in fact, many would argue that globalization has not just failed to alleviate want, it has even sharpened its bite.

Or:

> Globalization has not been the unmitigated panacea for global poverty that its more starry-eyed supporters promised; in fact, many would argue that globalization has not just failed to ameliorate want, it has even sharpened its bite.

Well, we have a 50/50 shot now, so that is already a victory. The correct answer is **E**: *Panacea* means "a cure-all," whereas *ameliorate* means "to make better." *Mediation* is "the process of promoting compromise," which doesn't quite fit this stem's meaning. *Alleviate* works fine in the second blank; it means "to lessen or make more bearable."

Look up *boon*, *exacerbate*, and *calamity* in your dictionary if you don't know the meanings of these words. If you're not a dictionary-user, you'll need to become one, as we'll discuss in a subsequent section.

PACING

A *set* is a group of items. We know that each set of Sentence Completions will be arranged in order of difficulty, and that ordering should help you strategize.

How does ETS know how difficult its items are? ETS "norms" its items by inserting potential items in experimental sections. It notes how many test-takers got them right, how many got them wrong, how many omitted them, and what all those test-takers' scaled scores were. It then constructs new sets from previously "normed" items, always listing them from "easy" to "hard." (There might be some fluctuation—an easier item may come after one of mid-level difficulty—but in general the trend is easiest to hardest.)

Knowing this fact can help you make judgment calls when tackling items. If you think you've got a good answer for an early-set item, most likely you're right. Don't waste time second-guessing yourself. However, if you see a seductive choice in a late-set item, think twice. These items tend to be nastier.

Don't take the order of difficulty in a set too seriously. An item's "difficulty" is a statistical quality based on the test-takers who encountered that item in an experimental section. It is *not* an essential feature of that item. You're an individual, and just because *most* test-takers found an item easy (or hard) doesn't mean that *you* will. So, while order of difficulty can help, you should follow what we call "Bombing Runs" in order to maximize your points in Sentence Completions sets.

Bombing Runs

Say your set has ten items. Begin by reading the first stem. If it seems easy, complete that item and move on to the next stem. If you encounter a challenging stem, skip that item. (Make sure to circle the entire item in your test booklet if you skip it. Also, enter answers in five-item blocks, omitting whichever you've skipped. You don't want to misgrid your answers.) After you've handled all the items that are easy for you— which may not mean the first half of the set, especially since you will have prepped for the exam—return to those items that you feel you could figure out, given a little more time. Make another Bombing Run, skipping all of the really tough ones. Repeat your Bombing Runs until time runs out.

If you approach Sentence Completion sets this way, you won't find yourself worrying over item number 3—which *should* be easy—for several minutes when you could have answered four other items. That's the principal error in standardized test-taking: wasting time on items you have little chance of getting right. You need to develop a fine-tuned sense of when to bail out on any given item. In order to develop this sense, you need to practice. Through practice, you'll not only learn more about the test and become an expert at applying the methods you've learned, but you'll also learn more about your own strengths and weaknesses. Are two-blank, logic-heavy Sentence Completions toughest for you? Or is it the one-blank item that relies heavily on difficult vocabulary? The more you practice, the more you'll learn…and the more you'll know about the test and yourself.

THE 6 MOST COMMON MISTAKES

As you tackle Sentence Completions, keep the following common mistakes in mind. Some are mistakes to avoid when taking the actual test. Others are mistakes to avoid during your preparation for the test.

1. Looking at the answer choices first, without having some idea of what the correct answer should be.
2. Spending too much time (more than a minute) on any one item in a set.
3. Failing to practice sufficiently—*reading* the book is not enough!
4. Failing to practice the step methods on every practice test item. You'll need these methods when the answer *isn't* obvious to you.
5. Refusing to fly Bombing Runs. That is, refusing to do items out of order based on your judgment of which will be easier and yield points more quickly.
6. Refusing to guess when you've eliminated one answer choice.

CONCLUSION

Without practice, you won't master Sentence Completions. You've learned quite a bit since you picked up this little book, but now comes the hard part—*you* have to apply it to testlike items. You'll find several practice sets at the end of this book. Here are some tips for getting the most out of these items:

- **Do not time yourself on the first set.** When you begin, don't worry about time at all. Take as long as you need to work through each set.
- **Read the explanations for all items, regardless of whether you got them right or wrong.** This last part is critical—always read *all* the explanations for each set's items. The idea is to develop skills that will help you get points as quickly as possible. Most important, just because you got a point doesn't mean you got it in the most efficient manner. The overarching goal is to apply the methods you've learned. Whether you get all, some, or none of the practice items right doesn't matter.

After the first set, you may want to start paying attention to time. Certainly, by the actual test, you'll want to give yourself about a minute or so per item.

ADDITIONAL ONLINE PRACTICE

Once you're done working through the items and explanations in this book, you can practice further by going online to **testprep.sparknotes.com** and taking a full-length SAT test. These practice tests provide you with instant feedback, delineating all your strengths and weaknesses.

Also, be sure to take the sentence completions posttest to see how well you've absorbed the content of this book. For the posttest, go to **testprep.sparknotes.com/powertactics**.

OTHER WAYS TO PREPARE

If you are not a reader, become one. Read literary fiction and magazines or newspapers with high-quality writing, such as *The New York Times*,

The Wall Street Journal, Scientific American, Harper's, Atlantic, The Nation, and *The Economist.* Many of these publications are available at your local library or free on the Internet. The most pleasant way to build up your vocabulary is by reading high-quality prose and learning by context.

You will also need to begin using a dictionary regularly. When you come across a word you don't know, treat it like a Sentence Completion: try to supply a word you do know to properly complete the sentence. Circle that word. Then, at the end of the day or week, look up all the unfamiliar words you encountered.

You may also want to read the *Vocabulary Builder* title in the *Power Tactics* series, which contains advice on word study, along with lists of words that have appeared frequently on recent SAT tests; lists of common suffixes, prefixes, and word roots; and exercises to build your vocabulary.

In your day-to-day writing, whether in assignments for school or emails to friends, strive to be exact and correct in your grammar, logic, and choice of words. Writing will help you to solidify your knowledge of language.

Finally, make sure you've planned out a schedule of study not only for Sentence Completions but also for all aspects of your SAT preparation. Having a plan and working day by day is the best antidote for anxiety. Preparing for the SAT does not have to be a nightmare. In fact, a positive attitude about the test will help focus your attention on maximizing your potential.

AND FINALLY . . .

In preparing for Sentence Completions, you will hone your grammar, logic, and vocabulary skills, as well as practice specific methods for answering these items correctly and efficiently. Remember, too, that in preparing for Sentence Completions, you're also preparing for the rest of the Critical Reading test. Paragraph- and passage-level item sets in this section depend partially on the sentence-level reading skills and vocabulary you'll be strengthening by reading this book. Much like musical proficiency, writing proficiency depends on having good role models (listen to the greats; read only the best writing) cultivating top-notch skills, and practice, practice, practice.

On to the practice items!

THE PRACTICE SETS

PRACTICE SET 1

1. Despite harsh punishments for fugitive slaves and difficult journeys through the night, Harriet Tubman proved her strength in the years before the Civil War by ------- capture and ------- many slaves along the Underground Railroad.

    (A) avoiding . . barring
    (B) allowing . . advising
    (C) eluding . . guiding
    (D) disproving . . abandoning
    (E) choosing . . defending

2. Throughout the past decade, the turnip crop has been -------, sometimes yielding abundant harvests and sometimes offering only meager quantities.

    (A) unprecedented
    (B) illusory
    (C) temporary
    (D) unstable
    (E) impracticable

3. As a painter, Raoul needs to improve his ------- skills; his palette is often striking, but his forms seem ill-placed on the canvas.

    (A) remedial
    (B) compositional
    (C) deductive
    (D) mnemonic
    (E) intuitive

4. Although the erection of the Berlin Wall in 1961 had been carried out -------, with the East German government making no public

announcement of its intention to seal the border, the wall's destruction in 1989 was ------- years earlier.

(A) zealously . . impacted
(B) warily . . acclaimed
(C) openly . . concerned
(D) hostilely . . approved
(E) clandestinely . . foreseen

5. The press misunderstood the politician's remarks about the economy; instead of taking them as -------, as the politician intended, the press heard them as defeatist.

(A) optimistic
(B) regulatory
(C) fiscal
(D) reliable
(E) indiscriminate

6. Although Rosa's apartment always seemed ------- to her guests, Rosa was not naturally ------- and had to make a great effort to keep her home in order.

(A) harmonious . . congenial
(B) nondescript . . understated
(C) immaculate . . fastidious
(D) impressive . . generous
(E) respectable . . vivacious

7. The advent of the compact disc in the 1980s relegated the vinyl record album to -------, making vinyl more important as a collectible than as a means of distributing new music.

(A) perpetuity
(B) obsolescence
(C) success
(D) renown
(E) infamy

8. Last year, the president of the company donated ------- percentage of her income to charity, a shocking generosity unmatched among other executives of her stature.

   (A) an incompatible
   (B) a paltry
   (C) a monolithic
   (D) an exorbitant
   (E) an unspoken

9. The magnificent antique watch demonstrated both technical precision and aesthetic skill; the watchmaker obviously possessed a ------- talent.

   (A) prodigious
   (B) lamentable
   (C) quotidian
   (D) tenuous
   (E) normative

10. Before the Vietnam era, the American government had seemed beyond reproach, a virtual citadel of -------, but the war and events like Watergate helped to tarnish that image.

    (A) dubiety
    (B) languor
    (C) temerity
    (D) usurpation
    (E) rectitude

ANSWERS & EXPLANATIONS

1. **C**

Forward Method

The introductory clause, *despite harsh punishments for fugitive slaves and difficult journeys through the night,* clues you in to the core idea of this sentence: that something occurred in spite of these two things. Continuing, you run into Harriet Tubman, who *proved her strength* doing something with slaves despite the two obstacles mentioned in the first clause. What could she have done? *Despite harsh punishments* and *difficult journeys* play off *capture* and *along the Underground Railroad.* You can predict that Tubman managed to *avoid* the punishment and complete the journey.

Now you need to check out the answer choices to see which one fits your prediction. Let's start with *avoiding*. *Avoiding* certainly works; hang on to **A**. *Allowing* doesn't work; nix **B**. *Eluding* works; keep **C**. Neither *disproving* nor *choosing* works, so both **D** and **E** are out. At this point, if you're rushed, you can plug the second word in both **A** and **C** into the second blank and see which has a better ring to it. If you have the time, you can ask yourself, Does either *barring* or *guiding* match the idea that Tubman completed the journey? *Barring* does not, but *guiding* does. You should double-check now to be sure that **C** fits the sentence: *Despite harsh punishments for fugitive slaves and difficult journeys through the night, Harriet Tubman proved her strength in the years before the Civil War by eluding capture and guiding many slaves along the Underground Railroad.* **C** is correct.

In this case, if you predicted "avoiding," *avoiding* in **A** would immediately seem attractive. But always remember to check both words, since often one of the words fits while the other does not.

Backward Method

If you didn't catch the logic of the sentence and weren't able to make a prediction based on it, you could still look at the word *capture* and ask yourself which word makes sense with it. Would *allowing, disproving,* or *choosing* work with *capture*? Not really. *Avoiding* and *eluding* both work, so keep **A** and **C**. Now check the second word of each choice against *many slaves along the Underground Railroad. Barring* doesn't work, but *guiding* does. It must be **C**.

2. **D**

Forward Method

Here, the main clause *the turnip crop has been* ----- is followed by *sometimes yielding abundant harvests and sometimes offering only meager quantities.* So you know the blank must be filled by something indicating that the turnip crop is sometimes one way and sometimes another. You can predict that the blank will be filled with something meaning "unpredictable" or "changing."

Looking at the choices, *unprecedented* means "never seen before"; nix **A**. *Illusory* means "imaginary"; scratch **B**. *Temporary* means "not permanent." Is that the same as "changing" or "unpredictable"? Might be a close call, so hang on to **C**. *Unstable* means "tending to change." Is that a better fit than *temporary*? Yes, so keep **D** and eliminate **C**. *Impracticable* means "not capable of being done"; out with **E**. Now you need to read **D** back into the sentence: *Throughout the past decade, the turnip crop has been unstable, sometimes yielding abundant harvests and sometimes offering only meager quantities.* **D** works and is correct.

Backward Method

What if you didn't see the connection between *turnip crop* and *sometimes...sometimes*? You could still cut down the choices by eliminating the ones that don't make sense in the real world. Would anyone be likely to say that *turnip crops* are *illusory, temporary,* or *impracticable*? Probably not. At this point, your best bet would be to choose between *unprecedented* (which could indicate that the harvests were bigger than ever) or *unstable* (which could indicate that the crops change from year to year). Now you'd have a 50/50 chance of getting a point for the item. Remember, the correct answer in SAT Sentence Completions always creates a sentence that could be said in the real world without sounding bizarre.

3. **B**

Forward Method

The main clause, *Raoul needs to improve his ------- skills*, is followed by *his forms seem ill-placed on the canvas*. What you need is a word that describes the ability to arrange forms. You might not be able to come up with a single word off the top of your head, but you know the idea you're looking for.

Take a look at the choices. Does *remedial* have anything to do with arranging forms? No; it means "supplying a remedy." Eliminate **A**. Does *compositional* have anything to do with arranging forms? Yes; it means "having to do with composition," which is the arranging of forms. Keep **B**. *Deductive* means "based on reasoning," *mnemonic* means "related to memory," and *intuitive* means "based on a gut feeling." You can get rid of **C, D** and **E**. If you read **B** back into the sentence, you get: *As a painter, Raoul needs to improve his compositional skills; his palette is often striking, but his forms seem ill-placed on the canvas.* **B** works and is correct.

Backward Method

If you didn't see the logic of the sentence, you could look at the choices and ask yourself which one(s) might be related to painting. The most likely choice would be **B**, *compositional*, because "composition" has a strong connection to painting. The others, if you didn't already know their meanings, don't have any apparent connection to painting, so **B** would still be your best bet for a guess.

4.   **E**

Forward Method

The introductory clause says *Although the erection of the Berlin Wall in 1961 had been carried out* ------- and is followed by a phrase indicating that the East German government said nothing about it. So we know the first blank will be filled by a word meaning "without public knowledge." The word *although* indicates that there will be a contrast in the sentence. So although no announcement had been made about the wall's erection, its *destruction in 1989 was* ------- *years earlier*. You need a word that will indicate that the destruction of the wall somehow contrasted with its secret construction. You can predict that the first word will mean "secret" and the second will mean "known."

Starting with "secret," scan the choices looking for a match. *Zealously* means "enthusiastically"; nix **A**. *Warily* means "cautiously"; get rid of **B**. *Openly* is the opposite of "secret," so eliminate **C**. *Hostilely* means "aggressively"; get rid of **D**. Does *clandestinely* mean "secret"? Yes. Even if you didn't know that already, the other choices don't work at all, so *clandestinely* must be the one. Read both words into the sentence: *Although the erection of the Berlin Wall in 1961 was carried out clandestinely, with the East German government making no public announcement of its intention to seal the border, the wall's destruction in 1989 was foreseen years earlier*. Both words work: **E** is correct.

Backward Method

If the logic of the sentence wasn't clear, you could still know that the first word had to describe the erection of the Berlin Wall and the second word had to describe its destruction. All the first words could theoretically describe its erection. So it would be better to look at the second one. You need a word that could reasonably describe the destruction of the Berlin Wall. *Approved* and *foreseen* are the best bets here. You can plug **D** and **E** into the sentence and see which sounds better. It's a 50/50 shot at this point, which aren't bad odds.

5. **A**

Forward Method

You know that the press *misunderstood the politician's remarks* and that they were taken as *defeatist* instead of what the politician intended. But what did the politician intend? The needed word will contrast with *defeatist*, which means "tending to expect defeat." So you need a word that means "tending to expect success."

Scanning the choices, *optimistic* means "anticipating the best possible outcome," so keep **A**. *Regulatory* means "relating to regulations"; scratch **B**. *Fiscal* means "relating to finances"; eliminate **C**. *Reliable* means "dependable"; get rid of **D**. *Indiscriminate* means "random"; eliminate **E**. The only choice that fits is *optimistic*: *The press misunderstood the politician's remarks about the economy; instead of taking them as optimistic, as the politician intended, the press heard them as defeatist.* **A** is correct.

Backward Method

You've read the sentence and it's not immediately clear how to proceed. First, the word *instead* tells you that you're looking for a contrast. A contrast with what? With *defeatist*. If you're not sure what *defeatist* means, you can still tell it's a negative word by its association with "defeat." So you're looking for a positive word to fill the blank. If you scan the choices, you'll see that only *optimistic* and *reliable* have positive senses. The other words (*regulatory, fiscal,* and *indiscriminate*) are pretty neutral. Now which word is better, *optimistic* or *reliable*? Which one contrasts more clearly with *defeatist*? Since the meaning of *reliable* doesn't really contrast with "defeat," you should go with *optimistic*.

6. **C**

Forward Method

The contrast here is indicated by *although*: *Although Rosa's apartment always seemed -------, Rosa was not naturally ------- and had to make a great effort to keep her home in order.* Both words here will contrast with *had to make a great effort to keep her home in order.* You know that Rosa is not naturally neat, even though her apartment always seems so. So you can predict that both words will be related to "neatness."

Scan the choices and compare each word to "neatness." Is *harmonious* related to "neatness"? No; eliminate **A**. Is *nondescript* related to "neatness"? No; eliminate **B**. Is *immaculate* related to "neatness"? Yes; keep **C**. Is *impressive* related to "neatness"? No; eliminate **D**. Is *respectable* related to "neatness"? Possibly, so keep **E**. You're down to **C** and **E**. Which is related to "neatness," *fastidious* or *vivacious*? *Fastidious* means "paying attention to detail" and *vivacious* means "lively." Of the two, *fastidious* is the better choice. Read **C** back into the sentence: *Although Rosa's apartment always seemed immaculate to her guests, Rosa was not naturally fastidious and had to make a great effort to keep her home in order.* **C** is correct.

Backward Method

Reading the sentence, you can figure out that it has to do with "neatness" because of *to keep her home in order.* So you should scan the choices and eliminate anything that doesn't have to do with "neatness" or the lack thereof. *Harmonious, nondescript,* and *impressive* don't have anything to do with "neatness," so you should eliminate them. That leaves **C** and **E**. Looking at *fastidious* and *vivacious,* you might not know the precise definition of either one, but *vivacious* has *viv-* as a root, which means "life" in Latin. Probably not related to "neatness." **C** is a better choice.

7.   **B**

Forward Method

The main clause says that the status of the vinyl album changed in the 1980s (*relegated the vinyl record album to -------*) and that it stopped being used as *a means of distributing new music.* You need a word that relates to the process of going from used to unused. It might be hard to come up with a single word right away, but keep the concept in mind when you scan the choices.

Does *perpetuity* relate to the process? No; *perpetuity* means "eternity." Eliminate **A**. Does *obsolescence* relate to the process? Yes; *obsolescence* means "the state of being outdated." Keep **B**. What about *success, renown,* and *infamy*? None of them is related to the process of becoming unused, so eliminate all three. Read **B** into the sentence: *The advent of the compact disc in the 1980s relegated the vinyl record album to obsolescence, making vinyl more important as a collectible than as a means of distributing new music.* **B** is correct.

Backward Method

If after reading the sentence, no prediction pops into your mind, you can still know that you're looking for a definition of the process of going from a current *means of distributing new music* to the state of being *more important as a collectible*. That sounds like a somewhat negative change, so you should scan the choices and eliminate anything that is clearly positive. Both *success* and *renown* are positive words, so out go **C** and **D**. *Perpetuity* is a neutral word, so **A** might not be the best choice. *Obsolescence* and *infamy* are both negative, so either **B** or **E** is likely to be the correct answer. Read both into the sentence and choose the one that sounds better to you. You're up to a 50/50 chance of getting it right.

8.   **D**

Forward Method

The main clause of the sentence tells you that *the president of the company donated ------- percentage of her income to charity*. The following modifier adds that it was *a shocking generosity*. The word *shocking* is what you're trying to match here. You can predict that the correct answer will mean "shocking."

Does *incompatible* mean "shocking"? No; eliminate **A**. How about *paltry*? No; eliminate **B**. What about *monolithic*? This one might be tough, so hang on to it for a second. *Exorbitant*? That might work as well, so hang on to **D**, too. *Unspoken* doesn't mean "shocking," so nix it. You're left with **C** and **D**. Read *monolithic* back into the sentence: *Last year, the president of the company donated a monolithic percentage of her income to charity, a shocking generosity unmatched among other executives of her stature.* Try *exorbitant*: *Last year, the president of the company donated an exorbitant percentage of her income to charity, a shocking generosity unmatched among other executives of her stature.* At this point you can use your ear and choose from the two for a 50/50 chance.

Backward Method

From the construction of the sentence, you can tell that you're looking for a word that has a similar meaning to that of *shocking*. *Incompatible, paltry,* and *unspoken* can all be eliminated because they don't convey that meaning. So out go **A**, **B**, and **E**. Looking at *monolithic* and *exorbitant*, you can plug both into the sentence and use your *ear*, guess for 50/50 odds, or you can use the word *roots* to figure out the correct answer. *Monolithic* has the roots *mono–* (meaning "one") and *–lithic* (meaning "stone"). A *monolith* is a large stone. Something *monolithic* is like a large stone. Probably not a good word for this context. *Exorbitant* has the roots *ex–* (meaning "out of") and *–orbit* (meaning "orbit"). Something *exorbitant* is "out of orbit" or, in modern terms, "out of this world." *Exorbitant* is a better choice. **D** is correct.

9.   **A**

Forward Method

The second part of the sentence describes the watchmaker's talent. You know from the first part of the sentence that the watch was well-crafted. So you're looking for a word that praises the watchmaker's ability. Something that says he *possessed* "an enormous" *talent*. You can predict the correct answer will mean "enormous."

   Prodigious means "impressively large," so keep **A**. *Lamentable* means "regrettable," so eliminate **B**. *Quotidian* means "commonplace"; eliminate **C**. *Tenuous* means "having little substance"; eliminate **D**. *Normative* means "relating to a standard"; eliminate **E**. **A** is the only choice whose meaning matches the prediction. Read **A** into the sentence: *The magnificent antique watch demonstrated both technical precision and aesthetic skill; the watchmaker obviously possessed a prodigious talent.* **A** is correct.

Backward Method

Here, you know you're looking for something suggesting the watchmaker had a lot of talent. You need a positive word. You can try to eliminate the words you know are negative or neutral, such as *lamentable* (notice the root word *lament*, which means "to regret strongly") and *normative* (doesn't sound either positive or negative). You can guess from the remaining three.

10.   **E**

Forward Method

The main clause states that *the American government had seemed beyond reproach*, followed by the modifier *a virtual citadel of -------*. You need a word that plays off *beyond reproach*. *Reproach* means "criticism," so you're looking for *a citadel of* "something beyond criticism."

Turning to the choices, *dubiety* means "the state of being dubious"; eliminate **A**. *Languor* means "lack of energy"; eliminate **B**. *Temerity* means "a heedless disregard of danger"; eliminate **C**. *Usurpation* means "the act of seizing control"; eliminate **D**. *Rectitude* means "moral uprightness." That's a close match with "beyond criticism"; keep **E**. Read it into the sentence: *Before the Vietnam era, the American government had seemed beyond reproach, a virtual citadel of rectitude, but the war and events like Watergate helped to tarnish that image.* **E** is correct.

Backward Method

If you're not sure what *reproach* means, you can still figure out that you need a positive word by looking at the subordinate clause *but the war and events like Watergate helped to* tarnish *that image. Tarnish* means "to dirty or blacken." The war dirtied the image of the government, so the government probably had a good image before the war. So you're looking for a word relating to having a good image. *Usurpation* probably won't be it; the root *usurp–* means "to seize"; eliminate **D**. *Rectitude* has the root *rect–*, which means "straight", so *rectitude* probably means "straightness." That's positive, so keep **E**. If you don't know the meanings of the remaining choices, you could guess or choose **E**, since you know it has a positive connotation.

1. Although special effects have existed in cinema for decades, today's special effects engineers have access to ------- that would have ------- their counterparts in years past.

   (A) technology . . amazed
   (B) knowledge . . regaled
   (C) creativity . . altered
   (D) largesse . . instigated
   (E) profits . . amused

2. Driven by her competing desires to further her political vision and to pursue music, Joanna ------- her goals and became an activist folk singer.

   (A) refuted
   (B) combined
   (C) disallowed
   (D) gauged
   (E) conceded

3. The mathematician's proof was so ------- executed that her colleagues had to concede that it was -------, yet another example of her powerful insight.

   (A) faultlessly . . imprecise
   (B) hastily . . judicious
   (C) sporadically . . meticulous
   (D) cleverly . . brilliant
   (E) improperly . . disastrous

4. His supervisor's comments ------- Luis, causing him to feel awkward and embarrassed in front of his coworkers.

   (A) excited
   (B) mortified
   (C) rejuvenated
   (D) calmed
   (E) gladdened

5. Naomi wanted to save money, but she found being ------- difficult when there were still so many places she wanted to travel.

(A) inflexible
(B) lavish
(C) dynamic
(D) frugal
(E) concise

6. As the year wore on, his study schedule, which was already -------, became so burdensome as to be completely -------.

(A) beguiling . . uncontrollable
(B) strenuous . . unmanageable
(C) unproductive . . discordant
(D) negligible . . purposeless
(E) impractical . . superlative

7. Not content to offer his readers a ------- account of his life in politics, Winston Churchill ------- a deeply penetrating look at the inner workings of government.

(A) meaningless . . disavows
(B) facile . . provides
(C) hurried . . constructs
(D) precise . . promotes
(E) capricious . . unveils

8. The food critic called the new restaurant -------, going so far as to describe it as -------; the menu, the service, and the décor had all been extraordinary.

(A) mediocre . . pedestrian
(B) preternatural . . déclassé
(C) glorious . . moribund
(D) irksome . . enervating
(E) astounding . . sublime

9. There was no need to send food supplies to the village after the devastating floods; the storehouses had been spared and the villagers had a ------- of grain.

(A) panoply
(B) regalia
(C) plethora
(D) bastion
(E) lacuna

ANSWERS & EXPLANATIONS

1.   **A**

Forward Method

The main clause, *today's special effects engineers have access to ------ that would have ------ their counterparts in years past*, plays off the idea that *special effects have existed in cinema for decades*. So, despite the fact that movies have had these effects for years, today's special effects engineers have access to something new that previous generations of engineers would have reacted to in some way. Since the sentence deals with special effects, especially with the difference between old-timers and newcomers to the field, the first blank probably has something to do with the ability to create the effects. You can predict that the first blank will mean "methods."

If you scan the choices, *technology, knowledge,* and *creativity* could work, so keep **A**, **B**, and **C**. *Largesse* (meaning "generosity") and *profits* don't work, so eliminate **D** and **E**. Now you need to deal with the second word. Plug *amazed, regaled,* and *altered* into the sentence and use your ear to guide you to the best choice. Only *amazed* gives the sentence a clear, logical meaning: *Although special effects have existed in cinema for decades, today's special effects engineers have access to technology that would have amazed their counterparts in years past.* **A** is correct.

Backward Method

If you didn't see the logic of the sentence right away, you could still narrow the choices down by focusing on the second blank. Which words could make sense with *would have ------ their counterparts in years past?* *Amazed* and *amused* could both work. You could guess between **A** and **E**, for a 50/50 chance, or you could plug the two choices into the sentence and see which sounds better. Plugging in **A** and **E**, only **A** makes complete sense: *Although special effects have existed in cinema for decades, today's special effects engineers have access to technology that would have amazed their counterparts in years past.* **A** is correct.

2. **B**

Forward Method

Here, you know that Joanna wanted *to further a liberal political vision and to pursue music*. You also know that she did something with those two goals and became an activist folk singer. Since becoming an activist folk singer incorporates aspects of both her goals, you can predict that the blank will be filled by something meaning "merged."

Now you need to scan the choices, eliminating any words that don't convey the meaning of "merged." *Refuted* means "proved wrong"; eliminate **A**. *Combined* could work; keep **B**. *Disallowed* means "forbade"; eliminate **C**. *Gauged* means "measured"; eliminate **D**. *Conceded* means "to admit"; eliminate **E**. Plug **B** into the sentence: *Driven by her competing desires to further her political vision and to pursue music, Joanna combined her goals and became an activist folk singer.* **B** is correct.

Backward Method

If you weren't sure what the logic of the sentence required, you could focus on the main clause, *Joanna ------ her goals and became an activist folk singer.* Which word could work with *her goals*? Scanning the choices, *disallowed* seems unlikely; eliminate **C**. If you know the meanings of the other words, you can see that **B**, *combined*, is the best choice. If you don't know the meanings of *refuted, gauged,* and *conceded*, you could still see that *combined* would work and choose **B**. You could feel confident in doing so because if an answer choice clearly works, no other choice will also work. **B** is correct.

3. **D**

Forward Method

The modifier *yet another example of her powerful insight* makes clear that the mathematician's proof was impressive. So you know you need to show that the proof was executed in such a way as to impress her colleagues. You can predict that the first word will mean "executed well" and the second "impressive."

Scanning the list for the first word, *faultlessly* and *cleverly* stand out, so keep **A** and **D**. The second words in the pairs, *imprecise* and *brilliant*, are pretty different, though. Which conveys the meaning of "impressive"? Only *brilliant*, so plug **D** into the sentence: *The mathematician's proof was so cleverly executed that her colleagues had to concede that it was brilliant, yet another example of her powerful insight.* **D** is correct.

Backward Method

You might not be able to predict exactly the type of word needed for either blank, but the modifier *yet another example of her powerful insight* tells you that the general sense of the sentence is positive. Which choices contain two positive words? Only **D**, with *cleverly* and *brilliant*. Plug **D** into the sentence: *The mathematician's proof was so cleverly executed that her colleagues had to concede that it was brilliant, yet another example of her powerful insight.* **D** works.

4. **B**

Forward Method

At first, you know only that the supervisor's comments had some effect on Luis. As you continue reading, you see that they made him feel *awkward and embarrassed in front of his coworkers*. So the missing word must convey the meaning of "embarrass."

Scanning the choices, *excited*, *calmed*, and *gladdened* are relatively easy to eliminate, since none means "embarrass." Get rid of **A**, **C**, and **E**. What about *mortified* and *rejuvenate*? If you don't know their meanings exactly, plug each into the sentence and use your ear to pick the better choice. If you know that "to mortify" means "to shame or embarrass," then you can jump right to **B**: *His supervisor's comments mortified Luis, causing him to feel awkward and embarrassed in front of his coworkers.* **B** is correct.

Backward Method

You can tell from the sentence that the supervisor's comments embarrassed Luis, so you know you're looking for a word that has a negative meaning. *Excited*, *calmed*, and *gladdened* are all positive words. Eliminate **A**, **D**, and **E**. If you know that the root *mort–* means "death" (as in "mortuary") and *juv–* means "young" (as in "juvenile"), *mortified* is a better choice than *rejuvenated*. You can also plug both into the sentence and see which sounds better to your ear, or you can guess for a 50/50 chance.

5. **D**

Forward Method

The introductory clause tells you that Naomi wants to save money. The following clause tells you she thinks it's difficult to do so. You know you need a word that means "able to save money."

Inflexible doesn't mean "able to save money"; eliminate **A**. *Lavish*? If you're unsure, keep it for a moment. *Dynamic* doesn't mean "able to save money"; out with **C**. *Frugal*? Unsure? Keep it. *Concise* doesn't mean "able to save money," so eliminate **E**. We're left with **B** and **D**. Try plugging each into the sentence and see which sounds better. If you know the meaning of the words, you know that *lavish* and *frugal* are close to opposites. *Lavish* means "spending extravagantly." Not what you need. *Frugal* means "cautious with money." Plug it into the sentence: *Naomi wanted to save money, but she found being frugal difficult when there were still so many places she wanted to travel.* **D** is correct.

Backward Method

If you weren't sure how to proceed with this one, you could know from the sentence that the word has something to do with money. *Inflexible* and *dynamic* don't seem related to money, so you could eliminate **A** and **C**. You could guess from the remaining three, which is still better than guessing from five. If you have the time, read each one into the sentence and see which, if any, clicks for you.

6. **B**

Forward Method

The sentence sets up a comparison between the study schedule at the beginning of the year and at the end. By the end it was *so burdensome as to be completely -------*. You know that the second word must mean something close to "burdensome."

Scanning the second word of each choice, *uncontrollable* in **A** and *unmanageable* in **B** stand out as possibilities. Keep them and eliminate the others. Now look at the first words of those two choices: *beguiling* and *strenuous*. Which is a better fit? We know that the study schedule had become even more of a burden than it *already* was, so we need a word that suggests "burdensome" again. Which is it? Try reading both choices into the sentence and see which sounds better. *As the year wore on, his study schedule, which was already strenuous, became so burdensome as to be completely unmanageable.* **B** is correct.

Backward Method

You know the second word is related somehow to "burdensome." The words *uncontrollable* and *unmanageable* convey similar meanings, so you can narrow the field down to **A** and **B**. If you don't have enough time to consider the first words of the pairs, you could guess from the two. If you have some time, plug in each complete choice and see which sounds better.

7. **B**

Forward Method

The main clause *Winston Churchill ------- a deeply penetrating look at the inner workings of government* follows the modifier *Not content to offer his readers a ------- account of his life in politics.* So the contrast is between *deeply penetrating* and the blank in the modifier. You know the first word must be somewhat opposite to *deeply penetrating*, like "superficial."

Scanning the first words, *meaningless* and *facile* stand out as possibilities. Keep **A** and **B**. Eliminate the others. The second words in **A** and **B** are *disavows* and *provides*. *Disavows* means "to deny." Does that work in the sentence? Did Churchill deny *a deeply penetrating look...*? No; eliminate **A**. *Provides* parallels *offer* in the modifier. Read **B** into the sentence: *Not content to offer his readers a facile account of his life in politics, Winston Churchill provides a deeply penetrating look at the inner workings of government.* **B** is correct.

Backward Method

The easier word to deal with is the second one, since it has to make sense with *a deeply penetrating look.* Which words fit the bill? Perhaps *provides* and *constructs*. If you're out of time, you can guess between **B** and **C**. If you have extra time, read each one into the sentence along with its mate. Which sounds better? You'll probably go with *provides* here. **B** is correct.

8. **E**

Forward Method

The main clause states that the *critic called the new restaurant* -------, *going so far as to describe it as* -------. The second part of the sentence lets you know that the restaurant is top notch. So the critic must have called the restaurant "great" and gone so far as to describe it as "wonderful" or something like that. The phrase *going so far as to* is almost always a sign on the SAT that amplification is involved.

Scanning the choices, the only words in the first column that mean "great" are *glorious* in **C** and *astounding* in **E**. The second word in **C** is *moribund*, which means "on death's doorstep." **C** doesn't seem likely. The second word in **E**, *sublime*, continues the meaning and takes it up a notch. Sounds good so far. Read it into the sentence: *The food critic called the new restaurant astounding, going so far as to describe it as sublime; the menu, the service, and the décor had all been extraordinary.* **E** is correct.

Backward Method

The word *extraordinary* tips you off that you need positive words here. You can scan the choices, looking for a pair of positive words. In the first column, *glorious* and *astounding* are possibilities. So you can guess from **C** and **E**. Or, if you sense that *moribund* in **C** is not positive, you can plug **E** into the sentence, see that it works, and move on to the next question.

9. **C**

Forward Method

The first part of the sentence lets you know that the village did not need extra food after the flood. The second part, containing the blank, explains that *the storehouses had been spared* and that the villagers still had grain. The blank, then, must mean something like "enough" or "more than enough."

Panoply means "a shining array"; eliminate **A**. *Regalia* means "the symbols of a rank, office, order, or society"; eliminate **B**. *Plethora* means "an excess"; keep **C**. *Bastion* means "stronghold"; eliminate **D**. *Lacuna* means "gap or empty space"; eliminate **E**. The only one that works is **C**: *There was no need to send food supplies to the village after the devastat-*

ing floods; the storehouses had been spared and the villagers had a pleth-ora of grain. **C** is correct.

Backward Method

This item is very difficult to handle if you don't know the words in the choices. You might recognize that you need a word that could be used with *grain*. Keeping that in mind, you could eliminate *regalia* if you notice that its root *reg–* comes from the Latin for "king." The others aren't easily identified by roots. You might need to plug them in and do your best with your ear.

PRACTICE SET 3

1. The highway construction project required more funding than the state could -------, so the highway commission proposed working in ------- private sources.

   (A) demand . . opposition to
   (B) renege . . place of
   (C) review . . comparison with
   (D) justify . . harmony with
   (E) allocate . . association with

2. Reacting to reviews that called his work childish and -------, the artist began his next series of paintings with a determination to convey maturity and -------.

   (A) irresponsible . . sincerity
   (B) meaningless . . simplicity
   (C) vulgar . . refinement
   (D) tedious . . generosity
   (E) obscure . . decisiveness

3. Siberian tigers are considered among the most ------- of animals; their striking coloration, powerful musculature, and aloof bearing leave many people -------.

   (A) fascinating . . defiant
   (B) anomalous . . fearful
   (C) splendid . . indifferent
   (D) disdainful . . perplexed
   (E) majestic . . awestruck

4. The accident resulted from ------- of unfortunate events; many factors came together to create the dangerous conditions.

   (A) a monopoly
   (B) a coincidence
   (C) a divergence
   (D) a repudiation
   (E) an elimination

5. Often ------- and -------, much of the country's workforce gets too little
    sleep and too little exercise.

    (A) cranky . . forlorn
    (B) vehement . . coercive
    (C) juvenile . . heedless
    (D) overextended . . flabby
    (E) exhilarated . . careful

6. Nguyen prided himself on his -------, an understanding of others'
    feelings that has earned him many friends.

    (A) empathy
    (B) temerity
    (C) astuteness
    (D) lethargy
    (E) sociability

7. The butcher, an especially ------- and devious man, often swindled his
    customers by rigging the scales in his shop.

    (A) furtive
    (B) bellicose
    (C) perceptive
    (D) emotive
    (E) diligent

8. Tonya's ------- in social situations became obvious when she offended the
    host by asking about his income at the party.

    (A) profligacy
    (B) mendacity
    (C) turpitude
    (D) gaucheness
    (E) severity

9. Though automobiles were relatively scarce in the first decades of the
    twentieth century, by 1950 they had ------- to the point of -------.

    (A) amalgamated . . invisibility
    (B) aggrandized . . ambivalence
    (C) proliferated . . ubiquity
    (D) evolved . . fruition
    (E) regressed . . dependability

ANSWERS & EXPLANATIONS

1. **E**

Forward Method

The main clause lets you know that the project *required more funding than the state could* -------. The blank here must mean something like "give." Your next move will be to scan the first word of each pair in the choices to see whether any match your prediction.

Demand, review, and *justify* don't mean "give." Eliminate **A, C,** and **D**. What about *renege* and *allocate*? If you know these words, you know that *renege* means "to go back on a promise" and *allocate* means "to distribute." **E** is a better choice. If you don't know these words, you can move on to the second blank. Since the state couldn't provide the money, *the highway commission proposed working in* ------- *private sources*. The second blank must mean something like "cooperation." Since you've already narrowed the choices down to **B** and **E**, you need to consider *in place of* and *in association with*. Which means "cooperation"? Only *in association with*.

Plug **E** into the sentence: *The highway construction project required more funding than the state could allocate, so the highway commission proposed working in association with private sources*. **E** is correct.

Backward Method

If you don't see the logic of the sentence right away, you can focus on the easier blank. In this case, the second blank is probably easier, since you need a word that can work with *working in* ------- *private sources*. You might sense that you need a choice that ends in "with" to complete the phrase *working in* ------- (with) *private sources*. Since **A** and **B** don't have "with," you can confidently eliminate them. At this point you can try to guess from the three remaining choices, or you can plug them into the sentence to see which works best. If you have time, you can also consider the meanings of the words *comparison, harmony,* and *association*. Which seems to make the most sense in this context? *Comparison* and *harmony* don't seem to fit as well as *association*, so you could choose **E** on that basis.

2.   **C**

Forward Method

The opening modifier, *reacting to reviews that called his work childish and ------*, plays off the main clause, in which the artist wants *to convey maturity and ------*. Since the artist's reaction to being called *childish* was to try to *convey maturity*, which is opposite, the two blanks must have opposite meanings as well.

Now you need to scan the choices, looking for pairs with opposite meanings. *Irresponsible* and *sincerity*? Do those contrast? Not necessarily; eliminate **A**. *Meaningless* and *simplicity*? Not really; eliminate **B**. *Vulgar* and *refinement*? Something that's *vulgar* is tacky and something that has *refinement* is elegant. These are opposites; keep **C**. *Tedious* and *generosity*? Not opposites; nix **D**. *Obscure* and *decisiveness*? Not opposites; eliminate **E**. Read **C** back into the sentence: *Reacting to reviews that called his work childish and vulgar, the artist began his next series of paintings with a determination to convey maturity and refinement.* **C** is correct.

Backward Method

You know that the review called the work *childish*, so the first blank is probably negative, too. Which words in the first column are negative? Well, they could all be taken negatively, so move on to the second blank. Since the artist now wants *to convey maturity*, he probably also wants to convey something else positive. Which words in the second column convey something positive?

Well, they could all be taken positively. So what to do now? Since *childish* and *maturity* are opposites, look for a choice containing opposites, as in the forward method above. Only *vulgar* and *refinement* are opposites. Plug **C** into the sentence: *Reacting to reviews that called his work childish and vulgar, the artist began his next series of paintings with a determination to convey maturity and refinement.* **C** is correct.

3.   **E**

Forward Method

The first part of the sentence simply states that *Siberian tigers are considered among the most ------ of animals*. The second part, though, states that the tigers have *striking coloration, powerful musculature,* and *aloof bearing*, which *leave many people* -------. So the blanks will convey more or less the same idea: that the Siberian tiger is striking, powerful, and aloof. Which words in the first column could convey this idea? *Fascinating*? Possibly; keep **A**. *Anomalous*? Not really; eliminate **B**. *Splendid*? Possibly; keep **C**. *Disdainful*? No; eliminate **D**. *Majestic*? Possibly; keep **E**. Now, among **A**, **C**, and **E**, which is the best choice?

Take a look at the second word in each choice and keep in mind that you need something that continues the idea of the first word. Does *defiant* continue the idea of *fascinating*? No; eliminate **A**. Does *indifferent* continue the idea of *splendid*? No; eliminate **C**. Does *awestruck* continue the idea of *majestic*? Yes; keep **E**. Read **E** back into the sentence: *Siberian tigers are considered among the most majestic of animals; their striking coloration, powerful musculature, and aloof bearing leave many people awestruck.* **E** is correct.

Backward Method

You might notice that the two blanks need to convey something positive about the Siberian tiger. You can scan the choices for a pair of positive words. The only pair that is positive for both blanks is **E**: *majestic* and *awestruck*. Read **E** into the sentence: *Siberian tigers are considered among the most majestic of animals; their striking coloration, powerful musculature, and aloof bearing leave many people awestruck.* **E** is correct. If you didn't see that both blanks needed to be positive, you could also ask yourself which word in the second column would be a realistic reaction to a tiger. *Fearful* and *awestruck* are both possible. At this point, you could read the full choices **B** and **E** into the sentence and use your ear to guide you. Or you could guess between **B** and **E** for a 50/50 chance.

4. **B**

Forward Method

The first part of the sentence tells you that the *accident resulted from a* ------- *of unfortunate events*. The second part tells you that *many factors came together to create the dangerous conditions*. So the blank must somehow convey the idea that the accident resulted from unfortunate events coming together to create dangerous conditions. You can predict that the blank will mean something like "happening at the same time."

Scanning the choices, which words could mean "happening at the same time"? *Monopoly* means "total control over the sale or production of a good or service"; eliminate **A**. *Coincidence* means "an occurrence of two or more events at the same time"; keep **B**. *Divergence* means "a departure from"; eliminate **C**. *Repudiation* means "rejection"; eliminate **D**. *Elimination* means "removal of"; get rid of **E**. Read **B** into the sentence: *The accident resulted from a coincidence of unfortunate events; many factors came together to create the dangerous conditions.*

Backward Method

If you're not sure what the blank should mean, given the rest of the sentence, you could plug each choice in and use your ear. If you notice *came together* in the second part of the sentence, you could know that the blank will somehow be related to that idea. Which choices could not onvey that idea? *Monopoly*, *divergence*, and *elimination* are all unlikely to be the answer. *Coincidence* seems to work, but if you don't know the meaning of *repudiation*, you might still go with *coincidence* because if one choice seems to work, no other could also work. But if you can't tell which is better, you could guess between **B** and **D** for a 50/50 chance.

5.   **D**

Forward Method

The opening modifier, *often ------- and -------*, contains two blanks that correspond to *too little sleep and too little exercise* in the main clause. So you need a pair of words that convey those meanings. You can predict the first blank will mean "tired" and the second blank will mean "out of shape."

Scanning the choices for the first word, *cranky* and *overextended* have the desired meaning, while *vehement, juvenile,* and *exhilarated* do not. So keep **A** and **D**, and eliminate **B**, **C**, and **E**. The second words of **A** and **D** are *forlorn* and *flabby*, respectively. *Forlorn* doesn't match "out of shape," so eliminate **A**. *Flabby* does match "out of shape," so read **D** into the sentence: *Often overextended and flabby, much of the country's workforce gets too little sleep and too little exercise.* **D** is correct.

Backward Method

At the very least, you can see that the second blank will have to correspond to *too little exercise*. If you scan the choices, the only word in the second column that seems to have an obvious connection to exercise is *flabby* in **D**. Plug **D** into the sentence: *Often overextended and flabby, much of the country's workforce gets too little sleep and too little exercise.* **D** works.

SAT POWER TACTICS | *Sentence Completions*

6. **A**

Forward Method

The sentence makes it clear that Nguyen prides himself on his *understanding of others' feelings*. You need to find a word that describes that type of understanding. You can predict you'll need a word like "compassion."

Scanning the choices, *empathy* means "understanding of another's feelings"; keep **A**. *Temerity* means "disregard of danger"; eliminate **B**. *Astuteness* means "keen judgment"; eliminate **C**. *Lethargy* means "lack of energy"; eliminate **D**. *Sociability* means "the quality of being friendly." This may seem tempting, but remember that you're not looking for "friendliness," but for "compassion." These aren't the same things; eliminate **E**. Plug **A** into the sentence: *Nguyen prided himself on his empathy, an understanding of others' feelings that has earned him many friends.* **A** is correct.

Backward Method

The sentence makes clear that you're looking for something relating to the ability to keep and make friends. You might not be able to pinpoint exactly what nuance is required here, but you can get a general idea of the word needed. Scan the choices and keep anything that seems like it could possibly work. *Empathy* and *sociability* are definite keepers (for future reference, remember that the root *–path* means "feelings"; the word "pathetic" doesn't really mean "loser-ish" but rather "inspiring feeling in others, usually pity"), so keep **A** and **E**. You can be fairly sure it will be one of those two, since the test-makers are not likely to give you too many choices that convey similar meanings, since they don't want you to be able to argue with the way they choose to define terms. You can plug each one into the sentence and see which sounds better. Or you can guess for a 50/50 chance.

7. **A**

Forward Method

You know that the butcher is *especially* ------- *and devious* and that he *often swindled his customers*. So you need a word, like *devious* and *swindled*, that fits in with the idea of the butcher as "dishonest."

Scanning the choices, *furtive* means "secretive"; keep **A**. *Bellicose* means "warlike"; eliminate **B**. *Perceptive* means "insightful"; eliminate **C**. *Emotive* means "exhibiting emotion"; eliminate **D**. *Diligent* means "willing to put in effort"; eliminate **E**. Read **A** into the sentence: *The butcher, an especially furtive and devious man, often swindled his customers by rigging the scales in his shop.* **A** is correct.

Backward Method

You know from the sentence that the butcher isn't an honest man. So the blank must be a negative word. If you scan the choices, you can comfortably eliminate *perceptive* and *emotive*, since they don't seem to say anything particularly negative about the butcher: these two words share the same roots as *perceive* and *emotion*, which are both pretty neutral. You can guess from the remaining three choices. Or, if you recognize that *bellicose* contains the root *belli-*, meaning "war," you can eliminate *bellicose* as unlikely to mean "dishonest," even though it is a negative word. You'd be down to two choices, *furtive* and *diligent*, which gives you 50/50 odds.

8. **D**

Forward Method

Tonya doesn't seem to have very good social skills, given her awkward behavior at the party. You can predict that you're going to need a word that describes an inability to know how to conduct yourself in social situations. Something like "tactlessness."

Scanning the choices, *profligacy* means "wastefulness"; eliminate **A**. *Mendacity* means "untruthfulness"; eliminate **B**. *Turpitude* means "lack of morality"; eliminate **C**. *Gaucheness* means "tactlessness"; keep **D**. *Severity* means "harshness"; eliminate **E**. Read **D** into the sentence: *Tonya's gaucheness in social situations became obvious when she offended the host by asking about his income at the party.* **D** is correct.

Backward Method

You can tell that you need a word here that describes a person's lack of social grace. But if you don't know the meanings of most of the choices in this item, it's hard to eliminate answer choices. You could comfortably eliminate **E**, because *severity* doesn't seem to fit. But if the other words don't have clear meanings to you, you can plug them in and let your ear guide you. It's not the ideal situation, but in tough single-blank items, sometimes you won't be able to do much if you don't know the words and you're better off making a guess and moving on to an item you can handle more easily.

9.   **C**

Forward Method

When an item begins with *though*, chances are you're dealing with a contrast. In this item, the contrast is between the fact that autos were *relatively scarce in the first decades of the twentieth century* and the fact that *by 1950 they had ------- to the point of -------*. So you need two words that will convey the idea that cars became more common after 1950. The first blank is probably easier to handle and will probably mean something like "become more numerous."

Scanning the first words in the choices, *amalgamated* means "mixed," so eliminate **A**. *Aggrandized* means "made more important"; eliminate **B**. *Proliferated* means "increased in number"; keep **C**. *Evolved* means "developed gradually"; eliminate **D**. *Regressed* means "returned to a worse condition"; eliminate **E**. The second word in **C** is *ubiquity*, a tough word most people are not likely to know, but since only *proliferated* worked in the first blank, *ubiquity* must be correct for the second. Indeed it is. *Ubiquity* means "the state of being everywhere." That works in the context of this item. Read **C** into the sentence: *Though automobiles were relatively scarce in the first decades of the twentieth century, by 1950 they had proliferated to the point of ubiquity.* **C** is correct.

Backward Method

The words in this item are hard, but you can eliminate some of the choices if you recognize that you need something that means "increased in number." *Evolved* and *regressed* don't seem likely to have that meaning, so you could eliminate **D** and **E**. Looking at the second blank, it seems unlikely that *invisibility* would make sense in the sentence, so you could eliminate **A**. It's down to **B** and **C**. If you have no idea of the meanings of the words, you have a 50/50 shot at a point by guessing.

PRACTICE SET 4

1. Vermeer's paintings were ------- by certain patrons during the artist's lifetime, but it was not until the nineteenth century, some three hundred years later, that he was universally -------.

    (A) collected . . praised
    (B) influenced . . rewarded
    (C) scorned . . promoted
    (D) relished . . dismissed
    (E) overseen . . guarded

2. Though the mayor claimed that he acted out of ------- when he ordered several new homeless shelters to be built, his critics maintained a more ------- view, insisting that the plans were actually to benefit a local contractor.

    (A) curiosity . . inaccurate
    (B) respect . . egalitarian
    (C) charity . . skeptical
    (D) frustration . . productive
    (E) determination . . complicated

3. Dante's *Divine Comedy*, written in three parts, is a ------- work that many people, daunted by the task of reading it in its entirety, often read it in its ------- form.

    (A) subtle . . universal
    (B) voluminous . . abridged
    (C) barbaric . . censored
    (D) morose . . unedited
    (E) tedious . . original

4. The dance program at the festival was -------, incorporating pieces from many different cultures and eras.

    (A) sporadic
    (B) impeccable
    (C) perilous
    (D) eclectic
    (E) lyrical

5. Candidates for public office often ------- popular views expressly to -------
    public approval, even though the candidates do not necessarily hold
    those views personally.

    (A) deter . . aggravate
    (B) denounce . . replace
    (C) sanctify . . arouse
    (D) neglect . . impeach
    (E) espouse . . garner

6. Humans have a tendency to assign personality traits to whole species of
    animals, saying, for example, that cats are ------- because they like to
    explore and that dogs are ------- because they enjoy the company of
    people.

    (A) inspiring . . reverential
    (B) inquisitive . . gregarious
    (C) uninhibited . . dour
    (D) jovial . . despotic
    (E) reticent . . nurturing

7. Despite her general -------, Gretchen could often be ------- with people
    when she felt stressed.

    (A) affability . . brusque
    (B) reliability . . imprecise
    (C) contentment . . relentless
    (D) tenderness . . erratic
    (E) animosity . . obtuse

8. Recipes for watercolor paint caution against adding too much pigment,
    lest the paint become -------, resulting in watercolors that are too thick
    and sticky to work with properly.

    (A) translucent
    (B) ponderous
    (C) malleable
    (D) glutinous
    (E) vitiated

9. The ancient Romans valued ------- greatly; they considered the ability to speak ------- a true gift.

   (A) kinetics .. speciously
   (B) egotism .. spontaneously
   (C) rhetoric .. compellingly
   (D) dialogue .. imperiously
   (E) poetics .. sincerely

10. An avid fan of mystery novels, Warren loved to solve the crimes and asked his sister not to spoil the mystery book she had just read by revealing details of its -------.

   (A) aphorism
   (B) epitaph
   (C) preface
   (D) denouement
   (E) metaphor

ANSWERS & EXPLANATIONS

1.   A

Forward Method

The main clause lets you know that *Vermeer's paintings were ------- by certain patrons during the artist's lifetime.* This is contrasted with the fact that *it was not until the nineteenth century, some three hundred years later, that he was universally -------*, which lets you know that the relationship between Vermeer and his patrons eventually expanded *universally*. What kind of relationship did Vermeer have with his patrons, though? A patron is someone who supports an artist, so you can predict that the first blank will mean something like "supported."

Scanning the choices, *collected* in **A** could work with "supported," so keep **A**. *Influenced* doesn't match; eliminate **B**. *Scorned* is the opposite of what you need; eliminate **C**. *Relished* could possibly work; hang on to **D**. *Overseen* doesn't really make sense with *supported*; eliminate **E**. Now you're down to **A** and **D**. The second word in **A** is *praised*, which makes sense in the context of the sentence; keep **A**. The second word in **D** is *dismissed*, which doesn't work. Get rid of **D**. Plug **A** into the sentence: *Vermeer's paintings were collected by certain patrons during the artist's* *lifetime, but it was not until the nineteenth century, some three hundred years later, that he was universally praised.* **A** is correct.

Backward Method

The main clause tells you about the relationship between Vermeer and his patrons. Since a patron is someone who supports an artist, you know you're looking for a positive relationship. You can scan the choices for positive words. Only **A** and **D**, *collected* and *relished*, have positive meanings in this context. You can guess from these two or consider the second word of each choice. In **A**, you have *praised* and in **D**, you have *dismissed*. Only *praised* is positive, so you can feel confident about choosing **A**.

2.   **C**

Forward Method

You know the mayor built some homeless shelters, claiming that *he acted out of* ------- in doing so, but that his critics, who are likely to mistrust the mayor, thought *the plans were actually to benefit a local contractor.* So you know that the critics doubted the mayor's given reason for building the shelters. The second blank is probably easier to handle here, since you need to show that the critics doubted the mayor. You can predict that the second word will mean "doubting."

Scanning the second words of the choices, only *skeptical* in **C** conveys the meaning of "doubting." The first word in **C**, *charity*, also works in this context, since the mayor was building homeless shelters, which he could easily claim as an act of charity. Plug **C** into the sentence: *Though the mayor claimed that he acted out of charity when he ordered several new homeless shelters to be built, his critics maintained a more skeptical view, insisting that the plans were actually to benefit a local contractor.* **C** is correct.

Backward Method

The fact that the mayor's critics think that the shelters were meant to benefit a local contractor should tell you that their view was probably negative. So you need a negative word for the second blank. If you scan the second words of the choices, *inaccurate* in **A** and *skeptical* in **C** stand out as negative. You can guess from these two for a 50/50 chance of success or plug them into the sentence and let your ear guide you. You might also notice that *inaccurate*, which means "incorrect," is paired with *curiosity*, which probably isn't right in this context.

3.   **B**

Forward Method

The first blank describes the book, which you know was *written in three parts*. The sentence then goes on to explain that *many people* are *daunted by the task of reading it in its entirety*. So the first blank should convey the sense of "long."

Scanning the choices, only *voluminous* in **B** and *tedious* in **E** have meanings compatible with "long." Keep them; eliminate **A**, **C**, and **D**. Now, for the second blank, the sentence lets you know that, because people are *daunted by the task of reading* the book *in its entirety*, they *often read* it *in its ------- form*. If they don't want to read the whole book, they probably read it in a shortened version. So the second blank should mean something like "shortened."

If you look at the second words of **B** and **E**, *abridged* and *original*, respectively, only *abridged* has the desired meaning. Plug **B** into the sentence: *Dante's Divine Comedy, written in three parts, is a voluminous work that many people, daunted by the task of reading it in its entirety, often read it in its abridged form.* **B** is correct.

Backward Method

If you weren't sure about the logic of this sentence, you could look at the first words of each choice and ask yourself which could be reasonably applied to a book. *Subtle, voluminous*, and *tedious* are all possibilities. Keep **A**, **B**, and **E**; eliminate the others. You could guess from these three, or plug them into the sentence and choose the one that sounds best to your ear.

4.   **D**

Forward Method

The main clause contains the blank describing the *dance program*. The modifier, though, tells you that it incorporates *pieces from many different cultures and eras*. So the blank must convey the meaning of *incorporating pieces from many different cultures and eras.* You can predict that you'll need a word that means "diverse."

Scanning the choices, *sporadic* means "happening now and then"; eliminate **A**. *Impeccable* means "unblemished"; eliminate **B**. *Perilous* means "dangerous"; eliminate **C**. *Eclectic* means "diverse"; keep **D**. *Lyrical* means "poetic"; eliminate **E**. Plug **D** into the sentence: *The dance program at the festival was eclectic, incorporating pieces from many different cultures and eras.* **D** is correct.

Backward Method

If you're not sure exactly what meaning the blank should have here, you can still eliminate some choices based on their incompatibility with the rest of the sentence. For example, *perilous* is related to "peril," meaning "danger." Not likely to be correct in this context. Eliminate **C**. Also, it's unlikely that you would describe a dance program as *lyrical*. Perhaps one of the dances themselves, but not the program. So you could eliminate **E**. Now you have a 1-in-3 chance of success if you guess.

5. **E**

Forward Method

The main clause tells you that *candidates for public office often ------- popular views expressly to ------- public approval.* You know from the last clause of the sentence that *the candidates do not necessarily hold those views personally.* So the candidates use those views to gain approval to win votes. So the first blank must mean something like "adopt" and the second "gain."

Scanning the choices, *deter, denounce,* and *neglect* don't mean "adopt," so eliminate **A**, **B**, and **D**. *Sanctify* and *espouse* might be harder to define, so keep them. Look at the second words in **C** and **E**. In **C**, you have *arouse.* Does that make sense in this context? Not really. What about *garner* in **E**? To *garner* means "to earn," which is compatible with "gain," your prediction. Keep **E** and plug it into the sentence: *Candidates for public office often espouse popular views expressly to garner public approval, even though the candidates do not necessarily hold those views personally.* **E** is correct.

Backward Method

You know that, in life, candidates for public office need to gain public approval to get elected, so you need a positive word in the second blank. Scan the choices: *aggravate, replace,* and *impeach* are not positive, so you can eliminate **A**, **B**, and **D**. Plug **C** and **E** into the sentence and see which sounds better. You might eliminate **C** on the grounds that *sanctify* has the root *sanct–*, meaning "holy," which is unlikely to be correct in this context.

6. **B**

Forward Method

The relative clause states *that cats are ------- because they like to explore and that dogs are ------- because they enjoy the company of people.* So you know you need for the first blank a word that means "likes to explore" and for the second a word that means "enjoys the company of people."

Scanning the choices for the first word, *inquisitive* in **B** and *uninhibited* in **C** are possibilities, Eliminate **A**, **D**, and **E**. Which is closer to "enjoys the company of people," *gregarious* in **B** or *dour* in **C**? Since *dour* means "glum and unpleasant," it's probably not the best choice. Eliminate **C**. Read **B** into the sentence: *Humans have a tendency to assign personality traits to whole species of animals, saying, for example, that cats are inquisitive because they like to explore and that dogs are gregarious because they enjoy the company of people.* **B** is correct.

Backward Method

If you didn't know the precise meanings of the words in the choices, you could still make some wise decisions based on your understanding of the sentence. You need a word to describe cats and one to describe dogs. The cats in the sentence *like to explore* and the dogs *enjoy the company of people. Inspiring* doesn't seem like a good choice for cats, so eliminate **A**. *Nurturing* doesn't seem like a good choice for dogs, so eliminate **E**. Now you're down to **B**, **C**, and **D**. You could guess for a 1-in-3 chance, or plug each pair into the sentence and let your ear direct you.

7.   **A**

Forward Method

Despite tells you right off the bat that you're dealing with a contrast item. So *despite her general ------, Gretchen could often be -------.* The two blanks will be contradictory. The word in the second blank applies to Gretchen when she feels stressed, so it's probably a negative word, something meaning "not friendly or nice." You can begin looking for the second word first.

Scanning the second words in the choices, *brusque* means "gruff." That fits your prediction, so keep **A**. *Imprecise* means "not specific"; eliminate **B**. *Relentless* means "unwilling to give up"; eliminate **C**. *Erratic* means "unpredictable"; eliminate **D**. *Obtuse* means "thickheaded"; get rid of **E**. Check the first word of **A**: *affability*. It means "friendliness." That stands in contrast to *brusque*, so **A** still looks like a winner. Plug it into the sentence: *Despite her general affability, Gretchen could often be brusque with people when she felt stressed.* **A** is correct.

Backward Method

Gretchen could often be ------- with people when she felt stressed should tip you off that this blank will require a negative word. *Imprecise* doesn't seem likely here, so eliminate **B**. *Relentless* could be negative, but probably doesn't make too much sense in this context. Eliminate **C**. That leaves **A**, **D**, and **E**. If you can't make further progress with the words, you can guess from these three. Or you can plug each pair into the sentence and see which sounds best.

8.   **D**

Forward Method

The recipes *caution against adding too much pigment, lest the paint become -------.* Become what? *Too thick and sticky to work with properly.* So you need a work that means "thick and sticky."

Scanning the choices, *translucent* means "allowing light to pass through"; eliminate **A**. *Ponderous* means "weighty and serious"; eliminate **B**. *Malleable* means "able to be shaped and molded"; eliminate **C**. *Glutinous* means "thick and sticky"; keep **D**. *Vitiated* means "made impure"; eliminate **E**. Plug **D** into the sentence: *Recipes for watercolor* paint caution against adding too much pigment, lest the paint become glutinous, resulting in watercolors that are too thick and sticky to work with properly. **D** is correct.

Backward Method

In difficult definition questions, it's often hard to eliminate choices if you don't have a sense of their meanings. In this item, you can probably tell you need a word that means "thick and sticky," but you might have trouble figuring out which choice has that meaning. Looking at **D**, though, you might see the root *glut–*, which resembles "glue." If you had nothing else to go on, you could choose **D** on that basis and you'd be right. You could also eliminate *translucent*, since *trans–* means "through" and *–ucent* means "shining," making **A** unlikely to be the correct answer. *Ponderous* has as its root *pond–*, which means "weigh" and makes **B** unlikely as well. Having eliminated two choices, you're in a good position to make a guess.

9. **C**

Forward Method

The first part of the sentence tells you that *the ancient Romans valued ------- greatly*. The second part tells you that *they considered the ability to speak ------- a true gift*. So you know that the first blank must have something to do with "speaking" and the second with speaking "well."

Scanning the first words of the choices, *kinetics* is "the science of motion"; eliminate **A**. *Egotism* is "selfishness"; eliminate **B**. *Rhetoric* is "persuasive speech or writing"; keep **C**. *Dialogue* is "a verbal exchange between two people"; keep **D**. *Poetics* is "the study of poetry"; perhaps vaguely related, but not close enough. Eliminate **E**. The second word in **C** is *compellingly*, which means "persuasively"; keep **C**. The second word in **D** is *imperiously*, which means "overbearing"; eliminate **D**. Plug **C** into the sentence: *The ancient Romans valued rhetoric greatly; they considered the ability to speak compellingly a true gift.* **C** is correct.

Backward Method

This type of question is extremely hard if you don't know the words, so don't spend a lot of time on it if you're not sure of the vocabulary involved. But you can still eliminate a choice or two to give yourself better guessing odds. Since the Romans *considered the ability to speak -------*

a true gift, you're probably looking for something positive for the second blank. *Spontaneously* doesn't seem positive or negative, so it's probably worth eliminating **B**. *Sincerely* is positive, but everyone has the ability to speak *sincerely* (except pathological liars), so it's unlikely that the Romans would have made a big deal of this. Eliminate **E**. As for the other three, if you don't know their meanings, guess from them. Or plug them into the sentence and choose the one that sounds best.

10. **D**

Forward Method

Warren loves to figure out whodunits and didn't want his sister to ruin the ending of the book for him. So you know the blank must mean "ending." Scanning the choices, *aphorism* means "witty saying"; eliminate **A**. *Epitaph* means "engraving on a tombstone"; eliminate **B**. *Preface* means "introductory statement in a book"; eliminate **C**. *Denouement* means "final outcome of the plot of a story"; keep **D**. *Metaphor* means "symbolism"; eliminate **E**. Plug **D** into the sentence: *An avid fan of mystery novels, Warren loved to solve the crimes and asked his sister not to spoil the mystery book she had just read by revealing details of its denouement.* **D** is correct.

Backward Method

This question will be very difficult to answer without some sense of the words involved, but you can eliminate at least one choice, *preface*, if you recognize the prefix *pre–*, which means "before." It's unlikely that a word having to do with "before" will give away the ending of a book. Beyond that, you can plug the remaining choices into the sentence and try to judge by ear.